GETTING INTO BANI

A selection of other titles published by How To Books

Achieving Personal Well-Being
Applying for a Job
Building Self-Esteem
Career Networking
Conducting Effective Negotiations
Coping with Self Assessment
Dealing with Your Bank
Delivering Customer Service
Doing Business Abroad
Doing Business on the Internet
Finding a Job with a Future
Getting a Job After University
Getting That Job
Getting Your First Job
How to Communicate at Work
How to Know Your Rights at Work
How to Manage an Office
How to Manage Computers at Work
How to Manage Your Career
How to Market Yourself
How to Return to Work
How to Start a New Career
How to Study & Learn
How to Understand Finance at Work
How to Work in an Office
Investing in People
Investing in Stocks & Shares
Learning New Job Skills
Making Decisions

Making Work Experience Count
Managing Budgets & Cash Flow
Managing Credit
Managing Meetings
Managing Projects
Managing Successful Teams
Managing Your Business Accounts
Managing Your First Computer
Managing Your Personal Finances
Managing Your Time
Managing Yourself
Mastering Book-Keeping
Mastering Business English
Passing Exams Without Anxiety
Preparing a Business Plan
Saving & Investing
Securing a Rewarding Retirement
Setting up Your Own Limited
  Company
Starting to Manage
Staying Ahead at Work
Surviving Redundancy
Thriving on Stress
Unlocking your Potential
Winning Presentations
Working Abroad
Writing a CV that Works
Writing a Report
Writing Business Letters

Other titles in preparation

The How To Series now contains more than 200 titles in the following categories.

Business & Management
Computer Basics
General Reference
Jobs & Careers
Living & Working Abroad

Personal Finance
Self-Development
Small Business
Student Handbooks
Successful Writing

Please send for a free copy of the latest catalogue for full details
(see back cover for address).

JOBS & CAREERS

GETTING INTO BANKING AND FINANCE

How to launch a rewarding career

Simon Collins

How To Books

Cartoons by Mike Flanagan

British Library Cataloguing in Publication Data
A catalogue record for this book is available from the British Library

© Copyright 1998 by How To Books Ltd,

First published by How To Books Ltd, 3 Newtec Place,
Magdalen Road, Oxford OX4 1RE, United Kingdom.
Tel: (01865) 793806. Fax: (01865) 248780.
email: info@howtobooks.co.uk
www.howtobooks.co.uk

Note: The material contained in this book is set out in good faith for general guidance
and no liability can be accepted for loss or expense incurred as a result of relying in
particular circumstances on statements made in this book. The law and regulations may
be complex and liable to change, and readers should check the current position with
the relevant authorities before making personal arrangements.

Produced for How To Books by Deer Park Productions.
Typeset by Anneset, Weston-super-Mare, North Somerset.
Printed and bound by Cromwell Press, Trowbridge, Wiltshire.

Contents

List of illustrations   8

Preface   9

1   Understanding how it works   11
      Modelling the financial system   11
      Making some basic distinctions   13
      Getting to grips with the numbers   14
      Updating the career idea   16
      Considering equal opportunities   17
      Summary   18
      Preparing for interview   18

2   Setting out your stall   20
      Taking an honest look at yourself   20
      Speaking academically   21
      Questions and answers   24
      Underlining your difference   25
      Changing careers   26
      Summary   29
      Case studies   30
      Preparing for interview   31

3   Motivating yourself   32
      Being realistic about money   32
      Sustaining the enthusiasm   34
      Living with pressure   35
      Thinking quality of life   35
      Knowing your reasons   39
      Summary   39
      Case studies   40
      Preparing for interview   41

4   Walking down the High Street   42
Approaching the banks   42
Looking at the building societies   47
Banking in the future   49
Questions and answers   50
Moving the big money: the fund managers   51
Exploring the public sector   53
Summary   55
Case studies   56
Preparing for interview   57

5   Getting into the City   58
Going in at the deep end   58
Understanding why it is there   59
Deciding from the start   61
Questions and answers   64
Sorting out banks   65
Cracking the stock market   68
Risking the exchanges   69
Summary   71
Case studies   72
Preparing for interview   73

6   Making the applications   74
Looking for vacancies   74
Sending off letters   77
Blitzing the market   78
Using the CV   79
Following up   80
Summary   80
Case studies   81
Preparing for interview   82

7   Interviewing with attitude   83
Forgetting about school   83
Dressing the part   83
Judging the style   84
Pushing the truth   85
Repeating the exercise   86
Keeping your cool   86
Summary   88
Case studies   88
Preparing for interview   89

8 Coping with rejection 91
Dwelling on mistakes 91
Appealing the sentence 92
Using the experience 92
Hiding the disgrace 93
Starting all over 94
Summary 94
Case studies 95
Preparing for interview 96

9 Striking gold twice 97
Getting more than one offer 97
Playing it straight 97
Burrowing inside 97
Predicting the future 98
Playing the auctioneer 99
Walking it out 100
Summary 100
Case studies 101
Preparing for interview 102

10 Making the most of success 103
Sharpening up 103
Getting around 103
Qualifying as a professional 105
Accepting bad news 106
Summary 107
Case studies 108
Preparing for interview 108

Glossary 109

Further reading 112

Useful addresses 114

Index 115

List of Illustrations

1 A model of the financial system 12
2 Total employment, UK financial system 15
3 The relevance of qualifications 22
4 Comparing starting salaries 33
5 Coping with stress 36
6 Quality of life 38
7 Global employment, the 'big four', 1997 43
8 The number of UK registered building societies, 1986–1996 48
9 UK institutional investors: transactions in financial assets, 1996 52
10 Foreign banks in the City, 1997 67
11 Interviews – what is going on? 87
12 Getting the best possible start 104

Preface

Not so long ago, careers in general and financial ones in particular started gently enough after school or university and trundled along until retirement. This book was written because this prospect is simply no longer realistic. For various reasons, not least the entry of women into the professions and dramatic changes in required skills, getting into banking and finance is not as straightforward as it once was.

This is not necessarily bad news, however! Fewer hard-and-fast rules about entry mean more flexibility on the part of employers, and you need not fit a particular 'type' to succeed. The fact is, whether you are a school-leaver, a graduate, or even someone already involved in an unrelated career, there is probably something for you in banking and finance. If only you could find it . . .

You are no doubt well aware that determination and skill are required to get the career you want. What may not be half as clear, as far as the financial world is concerned, is what sort of role is best suited to you, which employers you should aim for, and how you should approach them. The chapters that follow are dedicated to your success in resolving these questions.

Among the many people who put time and effort into getting this book into shape or to helping it along in general, particular thanks must go to Tim Dodd, to Tony and Sophie Stewart, to Lucy Camsey and, of course, to 'Major' Denis Brown.

Simon Collins

1
Understanding How It Works

MODELLING THE FINANCIAL SYSTEM

The world of banking and finance looks incredibly complicated from outside. The High Street **banks** and **building societies** may seem straightforward enough, but even there, once you start digging into what it is that they actually *do* with your money, it gets less and less obvious. And what they have to do with the stock market, the City, or how many dollars you get for a pound may be a total mystery.

If you are thinking about a career in banking and finance, it helps to know a little about what fits where. After all, it is called the *financial system* rather than the *financial systems*. Every financial institution is linked in some way to every other, and each type has a specific role. Having a general idea of the big picture will give you a good start:

- You will aim for the most suitable employers right from the beginning.

- You can see where a financial career could take you.

- It makes what specific employers actually do easier to understand.

Running through the model

There are plenty of academic books on the financial system, but they are daunting to read and usually contain far more detail than a general idea of the system demands. Figure 1 is a simplified picture that you may care to study instead.

The arrows represent the directions your money – everyone's money – can take. If you start at the box 'Your money' at the top left-hand corner of the diagram, you will see that not all of it need be part of the financial system at all. If you put ten pounds under your mattress, or buy a book with it (a 'non-financial investment'), it remains outside the system and it does not concern us further. If you

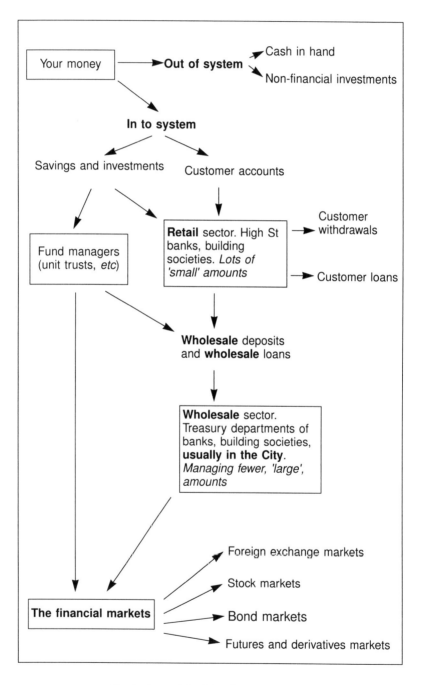

Fig. 1. A model of the financial system.

put this money in a bank or building society, or invest it in unit trusts, however, it is inside the system and this is where financial organisations come in.

You can see from Figure 1 that once inside the system, your money is either:

- saved and managed by professionals, or
- placed with your High Street bank or building society.

High Street banks and building societies are known as the **retail sector**, and they may lend your money back to people like you or bundle it up with the other deposits they receive and lend it on in large lumps to the **wholesale sector** of the system. Your bank or building society will of course keep enough ready cash in reserve for the normal needs of its customers.

The wholesale part of the system, as you can see from the diagram, is usually located in the City of London. Think of all the branches of your bank or building society taking in funds every day, bundling it up and lending it on to their central offices (usually called treasury departments) in the City. 'Your' part of those funds eventually finds its way into wholesale markets, where it is lent on once more to other banks or to large corporations. It may also support trading in financial markets, which banks and building societies use to try and generate supplementary profits.

Direct trading
There is nothing to stop you trading in financial markets directly, of course, say by buying shares. This has not been shown on the diagram as the amounts traded by individuals tend to be relatively small.

MAKING SOME BASIC DISTINCTIONS

One way of distinguishing between the retail and the wholesale sectors of the financial system is to call them **the High Street** and **the City** respectively. This is the way that most employees in banking and much of the financial press refers to them. The careers on offer in each are treated in different chapters of this book (4 and 5).

You may note from Figure 1 that the box marked 'Fund managers' lies outside this High Street/City division. A career in fund management, as we shall see, can combine elements of both High Street *and* City. But even here, an employee progressing from one to the other is rather unusual.

Why such a fuss about this distinction? It may at first sight look like pure conservatism, and you may wonder why everyone says that banking and finance is so dynamic these days, but think again.

Taking on new skills

The reason why you might need to choose between High Street and City is actually a rather practical one. Even if you know very little about what retail or wholesale banking involves, you might guess from Figure 1 alone that the skills you will develop over a career will differ depending on which side of the boundary you are on:

High Street employees
- are face-to-face with customers
- deal with local business
- cope with the financial needs of individuals and families.

City employees
- deal through the phone or computer networks
- speak to multinational corporations
- manage large sums and try to make them profitable.

Two different worlds
Part of the same system they may be, but High Street and City can at times feel like worlds apart. Most employers that have a presence in both places – the largest UK banks for example – interview for High Street and City posts separately.

GETTING TO GRIPS WITH THE NUMBERS

Banking and finance directly employs over a million men and women in the UK. That is to say that around one in 25 of the workforce belongs somewhere in Figure 1! Furthermore, this total has been remarkably stable over the 1990s. Banking and finance is sometimes described as 'financial intermediation' in government statistics, and you can see from Figure 2 how little the number of people employed has changed over this decade. If 'insurance and pension funding' jobs are stripped out of that total – the 'Fund managers' box in Figure 1 – we are left with jobs that could be referred to as banking pure and simple. These are also very stable in overall numbers.

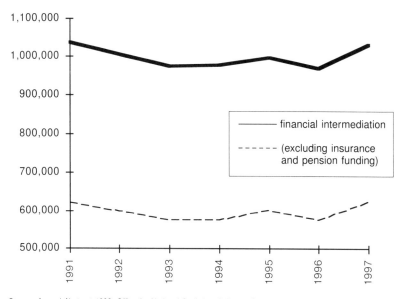

Source: Annual Abstract 1998, Office for National Statistics, © Crown Copyright 1998

Fig. 2. Total employment, UK financial system.

Reading between the lines

The totals make reassuring reading, but as always they can hide a lot. The truth is that the financial system has rid itself of a great many employees over the last decade, and has taken on different ones. The numbers may look fairly constant, but they don't represent the same people!

In the High Street and the City alike, machines have claimed a lot of tasks that people used to do. Most cash withdrawals are made via cash machines, for example. Telephone banking has grown, and so have direct debit payment systems. In the City, the army of clerks that used to process transactions has crumbled in the face of improved computer software.

So how come *total* employment has barely changed over the 1990s? There are two big reasons, both of which have a direct impact on what your career in banking and finance will look alike.

1. The range of 'products' that the financial system can offer is constantly growing. There are ways of saving, borrowing, managing and trading money that simply didn't exist in the past.

2. Banks and building societies in particular offer much more in the way of financial advice than they used to. The needs of individual and business customers are generalised less and personalised more.

If you consider the sorts of skills that used to be required to process cheques, hand out cash and work out interest payments, and compare them with what you imagine are needed for the newer sorts of banking and finance jobs, you can begin to see why staff turnover in the last few years might have been higher than it first appears.

UPDATING THE CAREER IDEA

The financial system of the past involved much routine work. Banking and finance careers, until at least the 1970s, had the following characteristics:

- Employees started off – and sometimes continued – in repetitious paperwork.

- Training was basic and restricted to the first few weeks on the job.

- Progression up the hierarchy had more to do with time served than ability.

- There was strict division between clerical and managerial grades.

- Once in, employees tended to stay.

No wonder financial careers held so little charm, and no wonder that bankers are still caricatured as being solid, boring, respectable citizens! All of the above applied just as much to the City as to the High Street, and it would be hard to say which part of the system had the least appeal.

The caricatures will last far longer than the realities. A career in banking and finance, as you may have guessed already, is not what it was:

- Computer skills are central to daily work.

- Training is flexible and it continues on and off right through a working life.

- Promotion is genuinely open in most organisations.

- Hierarchies have got much flatter – there are fewer ranks between top and bottom.

- There are no 'jobs for life' and many initial contracts are short-term only.

Putting yourself forward

If you imagine that a career in banking and finance will give you steady money with little required in return, you are well behind the times.

> **You are no longer looking at passing your working life in a sleepy backwater of the UK economy, but at being trained and retrained in a highly competitive, innovative, and flexible business.**

The sorts of things you do one week may be completely different from those you do the next. Thus even the word 'career' looks a bit old-fashioned. Your employment in a financial organisation may contain several different 'careers' following on from one another. Don't be put off by those who say that you're letting yourself in for a lifetime of total boredom! They've been staring at the caricatures too long. Boring it most certainly isn't, and as we shall see, if you are good at what you do you may find yourself shouldering significant responsibility before you have even left home.

CONSIDERING EQUAL OPPORTUNITIES

Tangling with statistics

Women make up just under half of all UK employees. The most recent breakdown by industry – that for 1996 – shows that women accounted for 46 per cent of employees in 'banking, finance and insurance', which is wider than our subject here but about as close as we can get (Source: *Labour Force Survey*, Office for National Statistics, © Crown Copyright 1997). There are not enough figures on the ethnic origin of employees to make a similar comparison.

Discriminating and the law

It may be that you never come across any discrimination, and that you enjoy a working life free from worrying about it. If you do suffer discrimination on grounds of your sex, colour or a disability, whether applying for a job or at work itself, you have recourse to law. Your local Citizen's Advice Bureau can help you to take matters further, or you may wish to contact the appropriate government commission directly. Addresses are given at the end of this book.

SUMMARY

1. Some general understanding of how the financial system works will help you apply to the right sort of employer from the start.

2. The retail part of the financial system is often referred to as the High Street, and the wholesale part the City.

3. Fund management does not easily fit into this retail–wholesale division.

4. High Street organisations and City ones are usually looking for different sets of skills. You may be very suited to one and not the other.

5. While total employment in banking and finance has been stable over the 1990s, there has been a significant turnover of staff within that total. It is less secure than it looks.

6. Careers in both High Street and City have changed a lot over the last 20 years. The advice of an older family friend on the subject is probably well out of date.

7. Your career in banking and finance is likely to involve frequent retraining and changes of direction as you go along. You will need to be adaptable.

8. If you are discriminated against on the basis of your gender, your ethnic background or a disability, you have recourse to law.

PREPARING FOR INTERVIEW

1. If retraining will be required of you on and off through a working lifetime, what does that tell you about the profession? Since when has change been boring?

2. Is there employment that is totally secure and also well-paid? Is there such a thing as a career that is interesting, yet risk-free? Are you disappointed that banking and finance is not as 'safe' an employment as people say?

3. Do you believe that women will achieve fair representation in the management of banks and other financial employers one day? Will this happen because of the good intentions of men, or because women get there by themselves?

2
Setting Out Your Stall

TAKING AN HONEST LOOK AT YOURSELF

It isn't easy! All of us are undoubtedly less coy about analysing ourselves than previous generations were, but whether we are more honest about it is arguable. We all like to be flattered, even though we pretend otherwise, and most of us tend to play up our good points rather than the bad. According to our own judgement, we are capable and even willing to do things which, in truth, we aren't.

Making the effort to go for any sort of job demands, as a first step, a well-founded conviction that you are willing and able to make a go of it. Obviously, self-delusion in this matter will show up somewhere along the line. Since most employment in banking and finance involves the screening and then interviewing of applicants by trained professionals, the chances are that you will be found out long before you get to sign a contract. The opposite holds true, too. If you really are the sort of person who could do well at the work, it may well show through even if you think you've 'blown it'.

Inviting the criticism

It isn't necessary to do a formal aptitude test or anything like that. Keep it simple. Ask friends, teachers, or tutors whether they think you could do the job in question. It may be that they don't know as much about the specifics as you do, in which case you can put it to them in a general fashion.

You aren't looking for a list of your faults. You are looking for people who know you and whose judgement you trust. You want them to tell you if they think that you are making a mistake, that's all. How many of your friends have taken career or other decisions that were absolutely *not* right for them? Don't fall into the same trap – ask somebody! We really can overlook the most basic things about ourselves.

Spending the time

A career decision should never be rushed. Unfortunately many of them are, and there is no shortage of unhappy people stuck in a rut because they jumped at the first idea that came into their heads. Banking and finance careers, like many others, demand not only that you show up for work at the appointed time every morning, but that you make the effort to learn and even study in your spare time. These days there is no question of drifting along with the mind switched off and going home when your hours are up.

Do yourself a favour – *think it through.*

SPEAKING ACADEMICALLY

As far as a prospective employer is concerned, the first indication of your ability is written on the application form under 'academic qualifications'. It's all very well going through school with the attitude that what really counts in the 'real world' can't be put down on paper, but the chances are that you'll never get to prove it. Academic results *count* in banking and finance, as Figure 3 demonstrates. They may not be the only things that count, and you're not necessarily lost if you didn't do very well in your exams, but if you're wondering whether a bit of extra effort at school or university is worth it, it is.

Worrying about maths

One of the most popular misconceptions about working in banking and finance is that you need particular genius in mathematics. Anywhere there is money, so the reasoning goes, there must be people with computer-brains handling it. Fortunately, the truth is a lot less forbidding, whether you intend to work in the City or a High Street bank.

You are not required to:

- work out complex multiplication faster than a calculator
- have been top of the class at maths
- demonstrate theorems of Euclidean geometry
- be familiar with the latest computer programmes.

You are required to:

- be confident and accurate in basic mental arithmetic
- demonstrate some objective proof of mathematical ability
- spot glaring errors that even machines can make
- have an open-minded willingness to learn new computer skills.

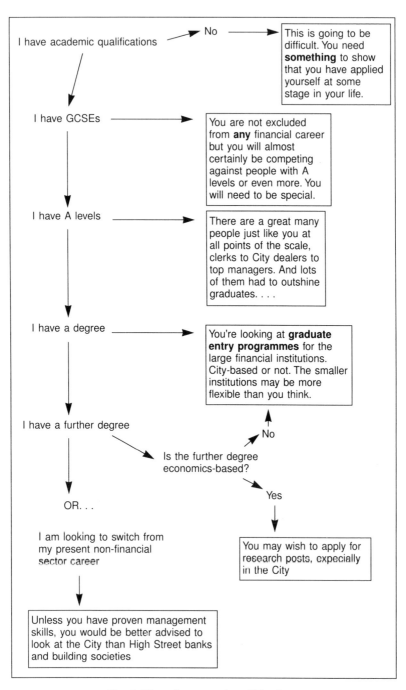

Fig. 3. The relevance of qualifications.

Nowhere is it written that you need an 'A' grade at maths A-level! There has been no mention of any specific maths qualification, either in this section or in Figure 3. All that has been said is that you need 'some objective proof of mathematical ability'. A GCSE pass in maths (or its equivalent) constitutes such a proof, and most institutions demand a GCSE pass at the very least from all prospective employees. They are not *obsessed* with maths – there are so many other things that go to make a success in banking – but they need to know that you are not frightened of numbers.

It is true that determination in particular circumstances can overcome the lack of formal qualifications, particularly in the City (see Chapter 5). It should be emphasised that this is very rare, and if you don't have any maths qualification you ought to think about getting one. Study in the evenings if you have to. The same applies to English language.

Studying specifics

Business studies and related courses have been popular at university level for some years. They are now common as A-level and GCSE subjects too. It is natural to suppose that if you study business or finance – at whatever level – you will hold an advantage when you come to apply for a job in a bank or a building society.

Not true! With the possible and special exception of the postgraduate **MBA** (Master of Business Administration, see page 29), it is not what you study so much as how well you study it:

• Most employers in the financial sector have some sort of training programme for people they hire. They don't expect you to know it all beforehand.

• There are many skills that will interest an employer more than business studies, even in banking – languages, for example.

• Good results matter far more than the subject matter. Good results demonstrate that you have the ability to learn and to apply yourself, general qualities that every employer is looking for.

By all means do a business studies or similar course *if it appeals to you in its own right*. The aim is to do yourself justice and to get good grades, and being interested in the subject will always help in this aim. Never choose an A-level or degree because you think that someone else will be interested in it! Do it because *you* are interested in it. The rest will follow on its own.

QUESTIONS AND ANSWERS

I didn't do as well in my A-levels as I'd hoped. If I'm thinking of apply-ing to work in a bank, should I do retakes?

It depends. Ask yourself why didn't you do as well as you hoped. If it was because you were going through a bad patch during the exams, or because you made a lot of silly mistakes which you're not going to make again, having another go may well make sense. If it was because you didn't study hard enough and the subjects didn't really excite your imagination, it's probably better to let it go. If you could-n't get involved over two years, it's hard to see why you would get involved all of a sudden and right now. Apply to the bank anyway. If your results are mentioned in an interview, be honest about them. Not everyone in banking is an academic high-flyer.

I've started a degree course in zoology but I have recently decided that I want to work in the City. Should I change to something relevant?

If zoology interests you, stick with it! You will get a lot more out of university if you are enjoying what you are doing, and your results will be better at the end of it. As for 'relevance', there is very little that is relevant to the City unless you plan to become an expert of some kind (economist, legal adviser, computer programmer). The City has traders who were Latin scholars, and corporate finance profes-sionals who could tell you all about stick insects. What they have in common are minds that can digest information and can play with it, and what these minds happened to be exercised on before the City is neither here nor there.

I did better in GCSE English than I did in maths, although I still got a pass in maths. Will that look bad to the building society I'm apply-ing to?

No! It's never maths above all with a building society or a bank. Your potential employer simply needs to know that you can handle num-bers – it's only reasonable! The building society you have in mind will be looking for a package of skills, of which maths is only a part. The fact that you have a good command of English is at least as important. The ability to communicate is vital in any business, and especially one where you will be in contact with a wide range of people.

UNDERLINING YOUR DIFFERENCE

Your academic prowess will only ever get you so far. Even if you have 13 GCSEs and three 'A'-grade A-levels, there is no guarantee that you will walk into a job in banking. What good academic results will do is get you over the first hurdle with relative ease. They won't necessarily help you over the second.

Putting studies in perspective

At some point your academic results will be old news. If they get you selected for interview, for example, you can't very well rely on them to get you a long way in the interview itself. Your interviewer will know that you did well. He or she will want to know what else you can offer, and you can't keep referring back to your grades. If you are under the impression that your advantage over other interviewees is engraved in stone, you will have a nasty surprise. Whether you got to the interview stage easily or not, you are all on the *same level* from there on in.

Getting involved

Let's look at it another way. You may know people who are excellent academically but who spend their waking hours with their books and who never talk to anybody. You may also know party animals who haven't studied anything for more than four seconds. Your instinct, if not your experience, will tell you that the first type may get interviews but have little chance of getting any job involving teamwork, and that the second would do brilliantly at interview – only they never get that far!

You should strike a balance. The pressure to study for longer and longer hours can be intense, but if you never get involved with something else *you will find it hard to get a job in banking or finance*. You need to do as well as you reasonably can in your exams, but you also need to demonstrate that you can get along with people and that you have other interests. Consult your common sense. Would *you* employ a top-of-the-class student who never laughs or goes outside? If you wouldn't, why would a bank?

Hiding your talents

Candidates for jobs in banking and finance are often reluctant to mention particular interests and abilities that they may have. They believe that their CVs and even their remarks at interview should be restricted to suitably serious and relevant occupations. Thus they say that they 'like reading the newspapers' or that they 'follow the stock market', and they leave out their involvement in amateur dramatics or their weekend motorbike trialling.

Don't hide what you have:

- Banks and other financial institutions are not as 'serious' as they first seem. They are run by people, not robots.

- Your interests outside the narrow world of finance will provide you with a certain balance and perspective. Good employers like these things.

- Diverse interests demonstrate that you are capable of getting on with different groups of people.

If you have a grand passion or hobby, mention it! It might be *that* difference that makes *your* difference.

Working for experience

Have you considered **work experience**? It is offered not only by the major High Street banks and building societies, but also by many of the larger City employers as well. Whether or not you intend to work in the end for the organisation that is giving you the work experience over your summer holidays, it is an excellent addition to your CV or application form. It not only shows that you know what your intended career involves; it demonstrates something of your initiative. See Chapters 4 and 5 for advice on getting such experience.

CHANGING CAREERS

If you are thinking of getting into banking and finance from another career, you are not alone. A significant number of people think about it, and more than a few manage the change successfully. Indeed, a working life consisting of two or more careers may become absolutely normal one day.

For the moment, however, there is no getting away from the fact that much of the financial system is geared around taking on school-leavers or students, training them up and attempting to keep them. As you may have noticed in Figure 3, you don't really fit into the majority of hiring programmes. You are still a bit of an exception.

Sorting positive from negative

Before you begin to think about who you ought to approach, and how, you should get your story together. You must expect some probing into your employment history and it's as well to have a consistent set of reasons for why you want to change direction. If you keep changing the reasons, or keep adding new ones, you risk giving the impression that you're not being straight. As for the reasons themselves, you might wish to bear the following guidelines in mind:

Don't include

• personal disagreements with your boss or colleagues

• moaning about how little you are paid

• criticism of the organisation or direction of your current company

• involved tales of office politics

• any domestic pressures.

Do include

• a wish to be involved with a wider range of people

• a desire to use your particular talents more fully

• generous acknowledgement of what your company has done for you

• some expression of enthusiasm and of willingness to learn new skills

• commitment to what you are attempting to do.

Being concise

There is no need to go over the top. No interviewer wants to hear a lengthy statement of all your reasons for changing, even if they are all good ones. Decide on a short and appropriate handful of points and stick to them.

Balancing experience and enthusiasm

Ideally, your CV will establish that you have experience. There should be no need to remind an interviewer of that fact, and if you keep doing so you will come across as a know-it-all or, worse still, as patronising. The key is to use the opportunities that you are given rather than launching into it all by yourself. Wait until reference is made to your experience and then capitalise on it.

An element often missing in would-be career-changers is enthusiasm. Your asset of experience will not help you if you come across as world-weary and cynical. There are dangers in being 'been-there-seen-it-done-it', but there is equally no need to be inappropriately immature and apparently *bursting* to change direction.

> **The ideal is an applicant who demonstrates a certain freshness and willingness despite having had something of a career already**.

Holding professional qualifications

Professional qualifications are *good news*. This may be obvious for people trying to get into financial careers who are chartered accountants, but it is also true for diverse professionals ranging from engineers to architects to medical practitioners. What applies to students under the 'Speaking academically' section above applies equally here. If you have a professional qualification, don't hide it. The qualities that got you that distinction can be used in other ways.

Selecting the approach

Heading out of your current career into one in banking and finance makes you a bit special. It is sensible, therefore, to consider your target employers particularly carefully. They are likely to be very different from those you might have approached if you had just left school.

City vs High Street

In general terms, you are more likely to find yourself a home in the City than in a High Street bank or building society because:

- High Street institutions are usually very large organisations that of necessity have standard entry procedures. With thousands of applicants each year, they have little incentive to struggle with special cases.

- Unless you are already a high-flying manager, it is not immediately evident what a High Street institution could offer you. Would you be comfortable on the same training programme as a teenager?

- City employers usually have smaller staffs than High Street banks. For many of them there is no standard hiring programme, and they consider *all* possible recruits as special cases.

- The City is proud of the diversity of its workforce. Employers *actively search* for people a little bit different.

- The City already boasts a number of individuals who have made finance a second career.

Taking the MBA

If you have the time and the financial resources, you might consider studying for an MBA – Master of Business Administration – when you pack in your first career. Most courses take one (academic) year to complete, and dozens of UK universities now offer them (see Further Reading at the end of this book). Courses are designed to familiarise you with the general principles of managing and analysing businesses.

The MBA is an Americanism that is gaining ground steadily over here, especially in the City. It's not a question of *needing* an MBA, but American firms in particular will take you very seriously if you have an MBA to your credit as well as a previous career. It marks not only your commitment to changing direction but also your ability to wrap your brain around the sorts of things that banks and other financial organisations are up to.

SUMMARY

1. Before you launch yourself into an application process, make sure that a career in banking and finance really is for you. If you're not sure, you'll be found out and it will be a big waste of time all round.

2. Don't rush your decision to 'go for it'.

3. The financial sector takes academic results very seriously. It is worth the effort to go one grade better.

4. You will struggle if you don't have a formal qualification in maths.

5. Your maths abilities don't have to be the wonder of your teachers, but you should be solid in the basics and comfortable with numbers.

6. Business studies and related courses at college or university do not necessarily give you any advantage when you apply to a financial institution, the particular case of the MBA aside. Do what interests you.

7. Good academic results will only ever get you so far. Be aware that at that point an employer will be looking for other reasons to employ you. Don't neglect non-academic interests!

8. Don't hide your interests and hobbies because you think they aren't 'serious' enough. Being well-rounded won't disqualify you from working for a bank.

9. If you are thinking of changing career, focus on the City rather than the High Street.

10. Career-changers might consider taking the MBA qualification.

CASE STUDIES

Tim is a 17-year-old accounts clerk

Tim should have done better in his GCSEs than he did. He works for a small accountancy practice in the London suburbs and is already thoroughly bored of it. He still lives at home and his frustration in what he sees as a dead-end job is beginning to fray not only his nerves but those of his parents and friends as well. He needs to get out 'into the world' and is dying to have a crack at a job where there is real interest and a chance of making a spectacular amount of money. The problem is that nobody seems to have any advice, apart from telling him to 'dream on'. He knows that his GCSEs aren't special, but he has confidence in himself and believes that given a chance, he can take it.

Alison is a 21-year-old student

Alison is about to graduate from an northern university with a degree in English literature. Expected to get a 2:1, and with a wide range of sports interests, she has a potentially impressive CV. The problem is where to direct it! She originally thought that she might teach, but has gone off the idea and is looking for a career that would take her to the bright lights of London and allow her to have some fun and decent clothes. She has travelled extensively around Europe as a student and had a lively time of it. Her ideal job would be one where she is surrounded by people, can assume responsibility, and yet afford some of the better things in life. The thought of settling down and marrying makes her cringe.

Roger is a 35-year-old, qualified civil engineer

Roger is married, with three young children, and has worked for Eastshire County Council for ten years. He was a promising student in his time but got onto the slow train somewhere and can't help feeling that better things await him than retirement. He also feels rather wasted. Most of his days at work seem to be taken up with picking stocks and managing his own modest portfolio. He takes a financial magazine at home and follows the business news with keen interest. He wishes he had thought of the City years ago and wouldn't mind knowing whether he is a bit late for all that.

PREPARING FOR INTERVIEW

1. If you don't really know whether you want to work in a given organisation, how would you handle your misgivings in front of trained interviewers?

2. Do you think of the world of finance as static or dynamic? How much use do you think a finance-specific degree is, if the subject-matter is constantly changing?

3. How much of customer relations in a bank or a building society, in your opinion, depends on mathematics?

3
Motivating Yourself

BEING REALISTIC ABOUT MONEY

Bankers have never been celebrated for their poverty. From the responses of job applicants, however, one might think that questions of earnings were the furthest things from their minds. Even in the City, talking about money – *your* money – is considered rather boorish. Of course it is a rare individual who works without wanting to be paid for it, especially when it involves putting on uncomfortable clothes and being confined inside all day.

Getting rich

There is money in banking and finance. Plenty of it. At one extreme, there are individuals in the City who earn hundreds of thousands, even millions, of pounds per year. Even at the other extreme the pay is by no means shoddy. The 16-year-old school-leaver just starting training in a High Street bank or building society can expect to be paid relatively well compared to similar posts in other employment and, of course, has every chance of making his or her way up a most rewarding scale in time.

The catch for those who want to become seriously rich, as opposed to merely well-off, is that the very large remuneration is reserved for a tiny handful. More often than not, the membership of this handful has a lot to do with being in the right place, at the right time; you can hardly rely on it happening to *you*.

Don't get carried away! If you work for a bank (or any other sort of company, for that matter), you are implicitly exchanging part of what you 'make' for a measure of job security. That is what an employment contract is all about.

> **Most of the seriously rich people you have heard of got there because they worked for themselves, not because they were employed. This is as true of the financial world as anywhere else.**

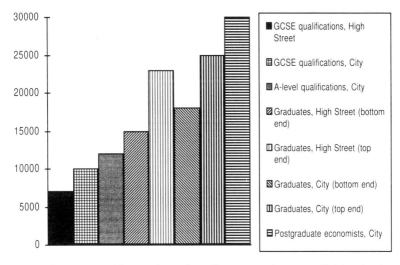

Note: all figures quoted in pounds sterling. All are approximate, unofficial and to be used merely as a guide.

Fig. 4. Comparing starting salaries.

Adding it up

So how much might you earn, in pounds and pence? Figure 4 compares some starting salaries, and although they have been averaged and rounded they give you a good overall picture. As for what happens after you have started, it's very much up to you. There are pay scales, of course, and industry averages for particular posts, but since your progress is not defined by how long you have been in place it's impossible to say that within two years you'll be paid X or Y.

Figure 4 shows that the City *generally* pays better than the High Street. It is not unusual to find graduates with three to five years' experience in the City earning £80,000 to £100,000, or about the most that top managers can expect in High Street organisations. But before you rush off to City interviews, remember that the money isn't 'free':

• City job security is very much lower than in the High Street.

• The City demands a working week that often shuts out *any* leisure activity.

• While there is stress in all walks of life, the City specialises in it.

- City careers are typically shorter than High Street ones, and the money may have to subsidise a second career.

- Around a third (on average) of City remuneration is paid as a bonus. This is entirely discretionary and you may suffer a run of 'bad' years being paid less than you expect.

Raising the issue

There are bold applicants who ask how much they will be paid if they are successful. There is nothing wrong with the question, and it's at least an honest one as it's what most of us want to know! The problem is that it's short-sighted. Starting salaries don't necessarily have a lot to do with how much you are paid later on, and certainly shouldn't have any bearing on a *career* decision. A better question would be what sort of remuneration you can expect over the next few years. This has the added benefit of making you look committed to the long haul.

SUSTAINING THE ENTHUSIASM

The less that our motivation has to do with our pay-cheque, the more likely it is that our enthusiasm for the job ticks along all by itself. There are careers where enthusiasm has little to do with being successful, but most banking-type careers are quite the opposite. This is probably due to the fact that direct customer contact is terribly important in a bank, and enthusiasm is one of the first things customers like to see.

Being enthusiastic at interview is one thing, keeping it up once you start working is quite another. If you have to wait for a train on a cold and grey November morning, enthusiasm will not necessarily be the first emotion that comes to mind!

Checking your own interest

Your enthusiasm for the job has got to be more than the thing you go on about at interview. Before you even get to an interview, ask yourself whether you are genuinely keen on what you're trying to do. If you *aren't* keen but you imagine that it will come once you get started, you are leaving an awful lot to chance. There are bound to be things in a new job that you can't take account of beforehand, but if you go in knowing that the everyday sort of work is likely to interest you, you have the right sort of motivation to start with. And you may well find that the financial rewards follow on naturally.

LIVING WITH PRESSURE

Plenty of careers involve some element of pressure, and banking is rarely free of it. The City dealer is notoriously stressed, the cashier in the High Street has to keep calm in the face of disgraceful rudeness. To some extent stress and pressure affect different people in different ways, but very few of us could keep a cool head in a dealing room where our year's profits are evaporating within minutes, or when we're insulted by someone we don't even know. We can all take just so much, but what decides how much 'so much' is?

Pointing at stress

Figure 5 may give you pause for thought. It may have occurred to you that there isn't really a separation between stress in a work environment and stress outside it. The sorts of people that get worked up in the Post Office or on the sports field are the same that throw calculators around, and those who remain calm when the keys get locked inside the house are those who can cope with difficult telephone calls. The amount of pressure you're under is something that *you* can affect.

Taking yourself seriously

Fortunately there's a great antidote to stress, one that gets better and better the more you practise it. The next time you find yourself getting hot under the collar at the bus-stop or in a supermarket queue, take a good look at yourself. Have a little laugh. How absurd you are! You laugh at other people getting worked up over nothing, so have a go at yourself, too. Does it *really* matter if you have to wait a bit for a bus, or even if somebody's rude to you? There are bigger things out there. Taking yourself too seriously isn't any good in a bank or anywhere else.

THINKING QUALITY OF LIFE

If financial gain is all that matters to you, you are (fortunately) a rare individual. Most of us have some conception of quality of life, which we balance against financial gain to assess whether a job or career is worth it. A poor quality of life demands relatively high remuneration, and vice versa. You would work on a boat in the Caribbean for considerably less money than you would require to work in a Siberian coal mine, for example.

Banking and finance lies somewhere between the Caribbean and

Testing your Stress Levels

Not every job in banking and finance is stressful, but individuals who are able to cope with it typically do better than those who are not. This could apply at interview or to those already in.

Be honest with yourself. There are no scores, but ring your responses and think hard about the number of 'Yes' rings. If you cannot cope with situations or yourself then you may have difficulty either enjoying a financial job or holding it down.

— Have I ever screamed at someone I don't know?	Yes	No
— Do I chew my fingernails?	Yes	No
— Am I afraid of speaking in public?	Yes	No
— Am I ever nervous about my appearance?	Yes	No
— Does waiting in a queue at the Post Office annoy me?	Yes	No
— Do I ever drink to get drunk?	Yes	No
— Do traffic jams really wind me up?	Yes	No
— Do I find it hard to take a joke?	Yes	No
— When I meet people, do I do all the talking?	Yes	No
— Do I refuse to let traffic out of side-streets when I'm driving?	Yes	No
— Do I jiggle my leg when I'm thinking?	Yes	No
— Do I care if somebody doesn't like me?	Yes	No
— If I apply for a job, do I need to know how much competition I have?	Yes	No
— If I couldn't answer an interview question, would it upset me?	Yes	No
— Have I ever panicked in a situation involving personal danger?	Yes	No
— Do I believe in lucky charms when I take exams?	Yes	No
— Am I unapproachable when I'm really bushed?	Yes	No
— Would spilling coffee on my clothes spoil my day?	Yes	No
— Are there people I know that I really hate?	Yes	No
— Do I ever wish that I was someone else?	Yes	No

Fig. 5. Coping with stress.

Siberia! Whether it's closer to one than the other is a matter of personal taste, but it's important to stop for a moment and figure out what your personal taste actually is. You should never choose a career for the sole reason that it pays well. You may think that decent pay is motivation enough, but it usually turns out that it isn't. Is there anything in Figure 6 that you recognise?

Redefining your wealth
Not all your wealth has something to do with the state of your finances. Look at wealth in a general sense and think of all the things you have that you value: friends, sports, your interests, your solitude. Try the following exercise:

1. Make a list of what you value in life, and exclude anything to do with your bank account from it.

2. Take each item in turn, and consider how a financial career might impact on it.

3. *Now* think of the money. Does it compensate for what you will lose?

Putting off happiness
Many people in the financial world reason things slightly differently from the above. 'Yes', they say, 'my quality of life is damaged more than I would have liked, and the money doesn't compensate me enough. But I plan to save enough to retire early and *then* I will enjoy a quality of life unimpeded by having to work at all.' Their motivation, in other words, is based on their intended future happiness, not on how they currently feel.

Don't copy their example. There's enough sadness around as it is.

- You can't do a job well that you dislike, and if you don't do it well the chances of retiring early will diminish all the time.

- It's very difficult to keep sight of a goal many years away if every working day keeps you away from what makes you happy.

- Unhappy working lives don't seem to produce happy retirements.

- Being young is precious. It isn't the same when you're old!

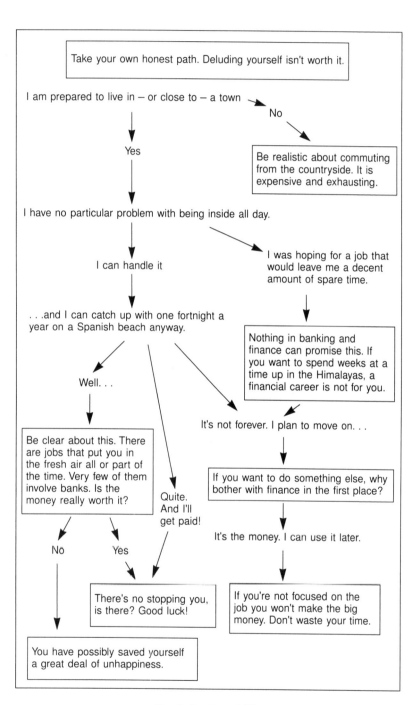

Fig. 6. Quality of life.

- Most people don't stick to their plan. They get stuck in a rut instead.

Striking the balance

In the end, we sacrifice something of our quality of life in order to get paid. The important thing is to ensure that the remuneration is *really* worth what you lose. Being motivated isn't just about the long term and thinking how happy we shall be when we have a big house and so on. It's also about enjoying the work on a day-to-day basis. This doesn't mean you aren't allowed 'bad days', but that in general you find your work interesting and fulfilling.

Think about your prospective career in banking and finance. It's not just the money that's pulling you in, is it? It's easy to say, 'I can get days off to do my rock-climbing whenever the weather's good', but you're deluding yourself, as Figure 6 emphasises. Money tends to just this sort of blindness. Keep your balance!

KNOWING YOUR REASONS

With any career, there are a whole lot of advantages and a whole lot of disadvantages all mixed up together. The relative importance of these 'goods' and 'bads' depends very much on your own personality, and nobody except you can really say whether the goods – principally, the money – are worth the bads. If this chapter gets you to take a good look at the possible negatives of a career as well as the positives, it's done half its job already.

As for the other half, defining the reasons why you are interested in trying for a job is a good exercise, for two reasons:

1. You may be asked for your reasons during interview.

2. If your motivation isn't sincere and thought out, it may all come apart.

SUMMARY

1. You will be relatively well paid in banking and finance, but you are unlikely to become a billionaire.

2. Don't choose a career, or between different employers in the same sector, on the basis of starting salary. It's only the beginning.

3. If your enthusiasm only extends as far as the interview, your over-all motivation is not going to be up to it.

4. Enthusiasm means wanting to do the job on a day-to-day basis.

5. Stress at work comes from the same place as stress elsewhere – your own mind.

6. Don't take yourself too seriously. You'll last longer!

7. Money is less motivating than you might think. Most people realise fairly quickly that there's a bit more to the equation.

8. Try defining your wealth in terms of non-money things. How many of these things will your intended career damage? The fewer, the better.

9. Don't fall into the trap of putting off your enjoyment of life to some unspecified date way in the future. Lots of miserable people do that.

10. Be clear about the advantages and disadvantages of the job. Don't just hope for the best.

CASE STUDIES

Tim is not naive

Tim can see that happiness has little to do with wealth. The prospect of being rich, however, is all the motivation he needs to pull himself out of his hole. It's not that he has expensive tastes, for at 17 he's not yet been introduced to any, but money would take him out of what he sees as the shabbiness of his current existence, away from the life-less rows of brick terraces and the stale sadness of every working day. Making money, for Tim, doesn't mean a loss of quality of life. It opens it up. He has absolutely no doubts, and a bit of stress wouldn't put him off one bit.

Alison realises what's valuable to her

Alison decides that no career is worth the loss of a social life, her tennis and rowing. She wants a good job, with promotion prospects and early responsibility, but employers that will require her to work as a matter of course from 7 am to 7 pm or later are not what she has in mind. In the final analysis, she doesn't care if job A brings her less salary than job B if it leaves her evenings and weekends free. She assumes that most graduates in most jobs get more or less the same sort of pay offers, and without having any particular figure in mind, she believes that she'll be happy with whatever the going rate happens to be.

Roger's motivation is intellectual

Roger's children are happy where they are and, although his wife would support him changing job, he is unsure what it might do to family life. He knows that his real interest – the stock market – is unlikely to keep him in Eastshire and would probably involve London. The commute would be around an hour, not counting a possible trip on the underground at the other end, and there wouldn't be much time with the children unless the whole family moved. The pay in a new career is barely relevant. Thus he decides to find out more, but considers himself uncommitted to a full effort.

PREPARING FOR INTERVIEW

1. Why do you think that multi-million pay-days in the City make headline news? Is it because they happen all the time or it is because they are unusual? Why should a bank pay you enough to buy a yacht in the Caribbean anyway, when it trains you, tides you over the years when you contribute very little and provides you with a whole raft of benefits in kind?

2. What's the difference between lightening up on yourself and being frivolous? How do you think you could blend professionalism and good humour in the face of stress? Why is it important to do it in a banking environment?

3. Do you know your own limits? What things about your life would you be really unwilling to give up? Do you think that they will be the same if you put them off until you're 40 or some other arbitrary age?

4
Walking Down the High Street

APPROACHING THE BANKS

The names are more than familiar. Take any British high street: if there isn't a Lloyds there's a NatWest; if there isn't a Midland, there's bound to be a Barclays. Only slightly less familiar would be Abbey National or Royal Bank of Scotland; drop down the scale and there might be Allied Irish Bank, say, or Bank of Baroda, large banks in their home countries but with relatively few branches in the UK.

Ask yourself why the High Street banks are there. Why the middle of town? It may be obvious to you that banks, like shops, need to be where people happen to be in order to attract their business. What may not be so obvious when you are thinking of a possible career is that these banks will involve you with people, real-life, unpredictable, annoying, and downright astonishing fellow citizens. All companies are fond of saying that you need to like working with people, but few can mean it as much as a High Street bank.

> **No matter the level at which you start, you will spend a remark- able amount of your training and then work trying to get on with strangers – the good, the bad and the ugly, people who smile, people who argue.**

This is really worth thinking about! There are individuals who revel in that kind of contact and others who could do without it first thing on a Monday morning. Before you put 'I like working with people' on your job application, be clear about what you are saying.

Naming the 'big four' banks

The **big four** need little introduction. They employ almost 350,000 people between them (see Figure 7):

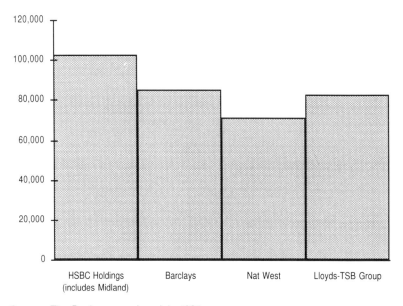

Source: *The Banker* magazine, July 1997.

Fig. 7. Global employment, the 'big four', 1997.

- HSBC Midland
- Barclays
- Nat West
- Lloyds-TSB.

Putting names to some other banks

Branches of foreign banks
In Britain's largest towns, especially those with established immigrant populations, you will find banks with head offices overseas and which attract business from the local immigrant community. For communities that keep strong links with their country of origin, such banks have obvious advantages. Among them might be:

- Allied Irish Bank
- Bank of Baroda (India)
- Bank Leumi (Israel)
- United Bank of Kuwait.

Private banks
There are a number of banks that cater specifically to the wealthy and who rely on a certain exclusivity and level of service to attract

their custom. Unsurprisingly, these banks are concentrated in London and may be British or foreign-owned. They may have just one office, and may be specialised departments of much larger banks. Well-known private banks include:

- Child & Co
- Coutts & Co
- Cazenove & Co
- Bank Julius Baer (Swiss).

Making sense out of clearing

You may have heard the term **clearing bank** or **clearer** bandied about as a synonym for High Street bank. The two things are not necessarily the same, and it would be a definite mistake to restrict 'clearer' to the big four High Street banks, especially since the gap between big four and the rest is getting smaller all the time. Either way, a prospective employee ought to know what clearing is all about before using the word in an interview.

Clearing is the mechanism by which the banks 'clear' their books with each other. If you bank with Barclays, for example, and you make out a cheque to someone who banks it at their Midland branch, there needs to be some mechanism that moves your money from Barclays to Midland. At the end of each working day, the banks total what they are owed and what they owe the other banks as a result of that day's activity. The net result of all those cheques, if you like. This net amount is 'cleared' (electronically) through the system. Without clearing, life would get complicated very quickly. Your Barclays cheque would only be of use to someone with a Barclays account.

The clearing system

The largest banks and building societies in Britain are all members of the Association for Payment Clearing Services. That is to say, they are all linked by the clearing system. Those banks outside the system participate by holding accounts – just like individuals do – with the clearers, and their clearing is organised for them.

How banks recruit

The clearers

Traditionally the clearers organised their employees into a great many grades of **clerical** and **managerial** staff. While it was possible to graduate from clerical to managerial grades, the two worlds were kept largely separate and you applied to one or the other depending on what academic qualifications you could boast. These days the internal worlds of our biggest banks are far more flexible, and there has been a tendency to reduce the number of grades and increase the variety of work experience you can expect.

Having said that, when it comes to recruitment there are graduates and the rest. When it comes to terms of employment, too, there are graduates and the rest, the former taken on as 'permanent' employees and the latter taken on initially at least on short-term contracts.

- Graduates are typically selected at the same time each year by a centralised interview process (which might involve some kind of written 'personality' test), and are destined for a fast-track training programme of several months. By the end of the programme the employee is expected to undertake management responsibility.

- Depending on the bank, it may be possible for an A-level entrant to get onto the fast-track programme right from the start. The clearers are more open-minded in recruitment than they might seem. More realistically, however, hopefuls who are not graduates need to enquire *locally* for details of recruitment. All of the major banks have ongoing recruitment needs, and school- or college-leavers have nothing to lose by simply walking into their local branch and asking for details.

- If you are serious about working for a clearer, and especially if you do not plan to go to university, work experience in a local branch is absolutely invaluable. Fortunately, clearing banks in general and the big four in particular have an excellent record in offering such experience. Usually this is organised through the careers offices of schools and colleges, but if you get no joy there, simply go into a local bank and ask.

Branches of foreign and private banks
Familiar names or not, both of these sorts of employer ought to be looked at as specialist institutions. Few of them have a regular hiring policy, and few will offer you the breadth of experience or the training of a clearer. Furthermore, in the case of working for a foreign bank, you are most unlikely to progress to management level unless you are appropriately 'foreign' yourself. Nevertheless, you may still be drawn to one or the other for your own special reasons.

If it is private banking that attracts you, you will find the International Private Banking Council (IPBC) most helpful. Over 40 private banks belong to the council, and further information is readily available upon request. The address of the IPBC is given at the end of this book.

Even if you wish to concentrate your career on a foreign or private bank, you might consider working for a clearer to get started. The training may be better, and you can gain valuable experience during the time it takes you to secure an opening in the bank of your choice.

Preparing to train

The clearing banks in particular have excellent training programmes, both for the graduate and non-graduate intakes. They are in a competitive market and are well aware that even their most humble employees can make all the difference between retaining customers and losing them.

Fast-track programmes

The **fast-track** programmes are not for learning how to order other people about. They are designed to immerse potential managers in all the detail of the bank's activities, and entrants are expected to absorb a great deal in a short time. They always include stints in the front-line of a busy branch, and graduates can expect to be shouted at by irate members of the public just like any of their fellow employees.

Basic training

Basic training for non-graduates is also varied. There are three elements common to our largest banks:

- assisting fully trained employees, usually on a one-to-one basis
- attending in-house training courses
- studying instruction videos.

Qualifications and training

Whether you are a graduate or not, training may lead you to professional banking qualifications, such as those offered by the Chartered Institute of Bankers (see Chapter 10). It is entirely possible that career advancement depends on it.

It should be obvious from the above that the major High Street banks take training very seriously indeed.

LOOKING AT THE BUILDING SOCIETIES

What is the difference between a building society and a bank? Until the mid-1980s the answer would have been a lot more obvious than it is now. Building societies were savings institutions which provided mortgages and were 'owned' by their customers. Banks were companies which provided a full range of financial services.

In 1986, however, the Building Societies Act lifted a wide range of restrictions on the activities of building societies, with the result that they have become almost indistinguishable from banks. In cases such as that of the Abbey National, the Halifax, the Alliance & Leicester, and the Woolwich, building societies have become legally recognised as banks. Indeed, at the time of writing, there are only two building societies left that have the traditional mutual structure and national coverage: Bradford & Bingley, and Nationwide.

Traditionally, building societies have appealed to job-seekers because they offered a more intimate and cosy relationship with customers than a large bank, and also because they did not necessarily revolve around head offices in London. Only a decade ago there were twice as many building societies as there are now, and their senior managers could claim with some justice that their staff had faces as well as names. Many societies still insist that such a spirit survives the recent changes, but in all honesty the claim is starting to look a little thin.

Wrapping up the history

The building societies on your High Street haven't finished changing. As they become more like banks, and compete for the same business as giants such as Barclays and NatWest, they have realised the need to become giants themselves. Mergers between building societies are a regular feature of the business pages. Figure 8 demonstrates just how many independent building society names have vanished in recent years. The merger between the Halifax and the Leeds Permanent in 1995 made a lot of noise; many of the others have not. If you are interested in applying to building societies for employment, you should keep up to date with who is buying who.

Concentrating the numbers

The High Street banks and the building societies have shown the same tendency to concentrate their activities. Although there might be branches of a half-a-dozen building societies down your high street right now it would be unwise to assume that they will all be there in five years' time. It makes sense, therefore, to approach building soci-

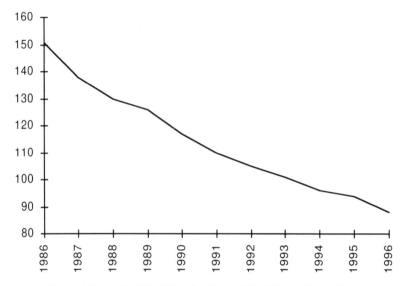

Source: 'Annual Abstract' 1998, Office for National Statistics, © Crown Copyright
1998

Fig. 8. The number of UK registered building societies, 1986–1996.

eties with the expectation that the work environment you start off in
is most unlikely to be that in which you end up. Whether you see this
as 'destabilising' or 'opportunity' is up to you.

Taking the time

An approach to a building society needs careful research. In the case
of recently merged societies you may have difficulty finding out what
the recruitment policy is or even who you could write to. This is not
to say that the effort isn't worth it; many building societies can offer
training and prospects that are equal to those of clearing banks and
even after merger many of them have a distinctly regional bias that
may appeal to you.

Concentrate your research into two areas:

- general business background
- investigating target building societies.

General business background

Any prospective building society employee, graduate or not, ought to
get up-to-date on what has been going on before taking further steps.

To be ignorant of a forthcoming merger or of the recent changes would look awful at interview. Remember that for the interviewer a prospective merger is probably the main subject of office gossip, and it will have an importance to him or her that is more than academic.

Reading back copies of the *Financial Times* at the local library is unnecessarily tedious and time-consuming, especially if you intend to go back more than a few months. An excellent substitute would be back copies of *The Economist*; the magazine will have missed nothing you should know and there is an index published every year which makes research much easier. Take notes if you wish; the most important thing, however, is to be aware of the general sweep of the changes rather than the detail of each merger.

Investigating target building societies
If you have a prospective list of employers in mind, you should check names and addresses before you send out letters or CVs. If the target is the product of a recent merger, there is nothing wrong with telephoning ahead to ensure that the personnel department is still at the last address you have. If you simply send out letters willy-nilly you run the risk of them never reaching the people you want them to.

BANKING IN THE FUTURE

No matter what technological changes may bring to the processing of money, and no matter whether the currency itself changes, building societies and banks alike will continue to be service industries, dependent above all on how their people cope with other people.

The skills expected of employees have changed, and individual banks or building societies may shrink or grow, but the profession as a whole has a future of enviable certainty.

Bearing this in mind, and also the fact that banks and building societies look more like each other with each passing month, you may be tempted to approach a career in a High Street bank or a building society without worrying too much about the particular institution you target. It is a sound long-term position, but for the present at least there are certain differences between banks and building societies that you should not ignore:

Banks	Building societies
Established career progression	Mergers may make careers unpredictable
Head office usually in London	Head office may well be in a provincial town
Established programmes for graduates.	Traditionally non-graduate recruitment among smaller societies.

QUESTIONS AND ANSWERS

It seems to me that graduates have got all the advantages even when it's my local bank they're applying to. I've got nothing more than GCSEs. Should I just forget it?

Absolutely not! After all, most of the people you deal with in your local bank or building society aren't graduates. It's true that graduates are usually taken on centrally and are offered permanent contracts straight away, whereas it may be that non-graduates have to apply locally and may be offered short-term contracts. There is still a bit of 'them-and-us' in those respects, but don't forget that they have to compete for the available jobs just like you do, and nobody is stopping you competing with them once you get inside!

Is the training that High Street banks offer all mathematical? Is it just like school?

This maths business! If you can get into a bank we can assume that you can count. Banks want employees who are professional, knowledgeable and personable. The training is geared to those ends, not to mastering the higher reaches of calculus. As for school, some parts of the training may mean that you have to study, or sit and listen. Other parts are far more practical. If that's like school to you then you'd have to put up with it.

Do non-graduates ever reach the highest reaches of management in High Street banks and building societies?

Certainly. Some institutions are more meritocratic than others, but in general the financial sector has a good record in spotting its own talent. Graduates get a head start in management because they have already proved that they can learn quickly and that they can apply themselves. If you aren't a graduate, it doesn't mean that you can't do what they can. It merely means that you need to prove it in your own way.

MOVING THE BIG MONEY: THE FUND MANAGERS

Perusing the pink pages

Take a look at the *FT* when you next get the chance and turn to the pages where all the previous day's prices are listed. Some of the headings will be familiar: stocks, foreign exchange, precious metals. What you may not have realised before is the space taken up with fund managers and unit trusts in the *FT Managed Funds Service*. Many of the institutions will be completely unfamiliar, and others will be familiar enough but with the words 'investment management' added on. The largest UK managers include the following:

- Mercury Asset Management
- BZW Investment Management
- Prudential
- Midland Montagu
- Hill Samuel Investment Management
- Invesco MIM
- Schroder Investment Management

In addition there are several non-UK managed funds which have a significant British presence, Fidelity being perhaps the best known.

Placing it all in context

All the above companies attract funds from investors and manage them in return for a fee. They may be owned by pension funds, insurance companies, or subsidiaries of banks, but they all do the same work and they are required by law to guard their operational independence. They are often referred to as 'institutional investors' and you might remember how they fit into the financial system from Figure 1.

You may be part of this world without realising it. Even if you do not buy and sell **unit trusts** directly, you may contribute into a private pension scheme or have some form of life insurance. Somewhere down the line your money is being managed, aggregated with that of lots of other people, and wielded in the world's **stock** and **bond** markets on your behalf. Fund managers play an increasingly important part in these markets, and fund management as a profession has

pushed its way into the front rank of financial careers over the last
two decades. Figure 9 gives some idea of the volume of transactions
that can be involved – *billions* of pounds each year.

Understanding the job

Fund managers as companies come in all shapes and sizes, and it is
dangerous to generalise. What is true of all of them is that they can
offer their employees a bit of everything. It may involve trading in
the markets, research, statistical analysis and a surprising degree of
personal contact with people outside the firm.

Most fund management roads lead to the City of London, although
Edinburgh has a significant presence too. The City is a hub not just
of UK finance but also of world finance, and fund managers, like
banks and many building societies, have found that it pays to be there.
Your insurance company may well manage hundreds of millions of
pounds in the world's markets, but it won't be doing it from your
High Street. Avoid confusing fund management with a career as an
independent financial adviser, by the way. We are talking here about
managing money, not selling life insurance policies.

The largest fund managers have graduate recruitment programmes

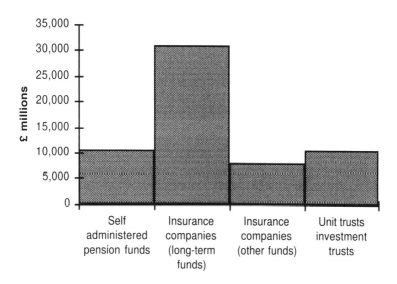

Source: 'Financial Statistics' Feb 1998, Office for National Statistics, © Crown
Copyright 1998

Fig. 9. UK institutional investors: transactions in financial assets, 1996.

and provide solid training for their employees. They all have opportunities for non-graduates, too, but you may find that hiring is irregular and unpredictable. As with so many other jobs, securing the vacancy that suddenly pops up has a lot to do with being on the spot at the time.

Making an intelligent search

As usual, graduates find the initial going a little easier than non-graduates. That is not to say that they face less competition for the jobs available, but at least there are established annual hiring rounds for some fund managers that they can try their luck at. Non-graduates need patience and determination.

Where to start?

- *Don't* send off CVs to every fund manager listed in the *FT*. It would be a thorough waste of effort and the list isn't exhaustive anyway.

- *Don't* wander into your local insurance offices and ask them for jobs in fund management. You need to understand that even the insurance company's own fund management arm will be constituted as a separate, arm's-length entity.

- *Do* scour the quality Sunday press job sections. Even if the jobs advertised demand more experience and qualifications than you have, write off anyway. If the fund manager concerned is hiring one person, they may well be hiring others, and you'll never know unless you ask. Somebody, somewhere, may applaud your spark of initiative.

- *Do* consult a reference work such as *The Investor's Chronicle Directory of Stockbrokers and Investment Managers* (see Further Reading).

- *Do* inform yourself a little about which funds are doing what and select a target handful in an intelligent fashion. Approach them by letter.

EXPLORING THE PUBLIC SECTOR

The Bank of England

'The Bank', or 'the Old Lady', isn't down every high street, of course. Its offices and employees (roughly 2,300 out of 2,800) are concentrated in the City, especially on Threadneedle Street, although it has agencies in twelve provincial centres.

The Bank is central to the entire UK financial system, the hub of the hub. It has several overlapping roles:

- It is the prime determinant of UK monetary policy.

- It acts as the government's 'strongman' in foreign exchange markets.

- It polices the financial system, in tandem with the Financial Services Authority.

- It licences the operation of banks and other financial companies.

> **Working for the Bank of England is possibly one of the most interesting and challenging ways you can earn a living in banking or finance**.

This is not a statement to be made lightly, but the Bank has an outstanding reputation for thrusting responsibility on those with the bottle to look for it. It can offer an extraordinary range of jobs within one career, and there is nothing like the prestige of being right in the middle of it all.

Recruiting
The Bank takes people on at GCSE, A-level, graduate and postgraduate levels. It also offers a small number of undergraduate final-year sponsorships and postgraduate studentships for economics graduates. There are minimum standards which you should reach before even thinking of applying:

- GCSE entrants – GCSEs should include 'C' passes at least in maths and English language.

- A-level entrants – require at least two A-levels or equivalent.

- Graduate entrants – require at least a 2:1.

Prospects

Once in, prospects are genuinely open, although graduates are started off on a four-year training programme and non-graduates are initially employed on clerical work. If you are good enough, you can catch up no matter where you start.

Of course, there's a hitch! Two of them, to be precise, although it may be that for you these aren't really catches at all:

• There are a great deal of applicants for each position available.

• In general, the Bank can't pay the kind of money that's sometimes on offer in the City's private sector. It has to be said that Bank staff have been known to move to more prosperous pastures.

The Department of National Savings

Ironically, National Savings wouldn't usually roll off the tongue in a list of High Street institutions, but Premium Bonds have become part of British folklore. Walk into your local Post Office, and National Savings posters and leaflets will be in plain view; not just Premium Bonds, but a variety of savings ideas that offer attractive rates of return and which are backed by the financial weight of the government itself. It is the job of the Department of National Savings to market and administer these savings ideas.

The Department is not part of the Post Office, but an Executive Agency of the Chancellor of the Exchequer. Its approximately 4,500 staff are Civil Servants and are taken on, paid and graded according to Home Civil Service guidelines. The Department advertises vacancies in Jobcentres and the local press, and like the rest of the Civil Service, you may approach them directly for information and application forms. Their staff are concentrated in London, Glasgow, Durham and the Blackpool area.

SUMMARY

1. The largest High Street banks are clearing banks.

2. There are limitations in employment with foreign or private High Street banks.

3. High Street banks and building societies require you to like working with people – not just *saying* it but *meaning* it.

4. Building societies are undergoing rapid change and look more and more like banks. Every prospective employee ought to be up-to-date with developments.

5. The clearing banks and the largest building societies offer excellent training, usually including a fast-track scheme for graduates.

6. Fund management is a growing source of employment but often requires effort on your part to find out who is hiring and when.

7. The Bank of England is not exclusively for postgraduate entrants. It has a significant non-graduate entry and promotion is genuinely open to all.

8. Don't overlook the Department of National Savings, especially if you want to steer clear of London.

CASE STUDIES

Tim asks for information
The idea occurs to Tim as he sits in front of the television news one dull evening. The office has been particularly petty that day and he can't help contrasting his work with that of the people he sees making the news. There is an item about an unfolding financial crisis; men and women are filmed walking purposefully out of the Bank of England and being whisked away in waiting cars. How did *they* get to do *that*? He finds himself wishing that he could be at the centre of things, with Jaguars waiting to take *him* to meetings with the Chancellor or whoever. Then the idea comes and he can't shake it off. Who gets to work at the Bank of England? Nobody he knows can tell him. For once, he thinks, he's going to act. He calls directory enquiries, and gets the number he wants. Easy. The next day the Bank of England tells him that it will send him all the careers information he could possibly want.

Alison warms to the idea of personnel management
A presentation at university by a big four bank wouldn't normally be Alison's cup of tea, but the word is out that they lay on plenty of food and drink and one of her friends is going anyway. She's got nothing on at lunchtime and so she agrees to show up. She listens to what is said with interest, and happens to fall into conversation with one of the speakers over a glass of wine afterwards – a woman who is

bubbly, amusing and happy. Her badge says 'Personnel' on it and Alison asks what it's all about. It isn't at all what she thought of as banking.

Roger defines his targets

Nothing if not systematic, Roger makes lists. He writes down the things he might like to do: trading stocks, trading bonds, managing portfolios. He then writes down the names of all the institutions that he thinks might be involved in one or more of these activities. He adds to the names he knows off the top of his head by consulting reference works and the *FT* in the local library. He then crosses out all those that have no office in or close to Eastshire, by referring to the telephone books. He is left with half-a-dozen company names, a local stockbroker and companies involved with fund management. He resolves to drive to each of them, just to take a look. Are they large offices, or simply local branches of big London institutions?

PREPARING FOR INTERVIEW

1. Have you ever lost your cool with a bank teller or manager? How often do you think that these people have to cope with angry customers? Could *you* subdue upset people?

2. Do you think that increasing automation of payments and the financial system in general will lead to a reduction in the number of employees in High Street banks and building societies? Why do *you* bank where you do? If your local manager was replaced by a computer, would you care?

3. When you save money or buy life insurance, have you ever considered what happens to your money? Do you know where it is invested and who decided it should go there? Is it something *you* could decide?

5
Getting into the City

GOING IN AT THE DEEP END

In the crush of converted warehouses and shining glass towers that we call the Square Mile lives an incredible assortment of financial companies. The City these days is not confined to the old boundaries of the City of London, although it is still concentrated there. It has outposts in the Docklands and even in the West End, but for all that the traditional geographical names are still used.

The City is unarguably one of the hubs of the world's financial system, and in some respects can be called the most important of them all. It's no excuse for being timid about applying for jobs there! It is going in at the deep end, but it's not as forbidding as it might seem:

- Almost everyone who works in the City will tell you that they knew very little about their prospective employers when they started looking.

- A school- or university-leaver will not normally be expected to know the nuts and bolts of who does what. The City is principally looking at *ability*, not knowledge. Employers can't give you the first, but they can work on the second.

- By having a reasonable idea about what sort of thing you'd like to do, and what sort of employer would suit you, you can cut right down on the number of potential targets.

- A good number of City employers offer work experience. If this appeals to you, apply early. It is popular.

Jumping the gap

If it seems like a good idea to you to start off in a High Street bank or building society and then apply to jobs in the City on the basis of your experience, you might remember from Chapter 1 that the skills required to work in each part of the system can be rather different. That applies to Lloyds, Abbey National and the rest of them as much as it does to Merrill Lynch or Deutsche Bank.

While there is nothing stopping you applying for jobs in the City if you already work for a High Street bank or building society, you are unlikely to hold any advantage over those who have worked in some other type of company. You will find that the vast majority of employees of UK clearing banks who work in the City were hired in the City, not transferred from High Street branches.

There really isn't an easy way in, and the gap is bigger than it looks.

> **If you want to work in the City, you should apply to the City, not beat about the bush.**

Waiting in the wings

There's another type of beating about the bush: working for some 'peripheral' City company – in telecommunications, say, or in computer servicing – in the belief that being near the heart of things will enable you to spot opportunities before anybody else. The same principle applies – *apply to where you want to work, not somewhere else.* You will do yourself no favours by getting stuck on the wrong set of rails.

UNDERSTANDING WHY IT IS THERE

This isn't a textbook, but you might find it helpful to expand your basic understanding of what the City is about. Placing the City in context usually dispels a good part of the fog that hides it from outsiders.

The wholesale end

Turn back to Figure 1, the basic model used in Chapter 1. The first essential about the City is that it is a **wholesale** centre, not a **retail** one. Imagine all the High Street accounts, and all the loans and deposits outstanding with each bank or building society. Imagine what kind of amounts might be involved, especially if you remember that businesses as well as individuals borrow and deposit money. How are these funds managed? Where is it decided what interest rates to charge or pay out, and how does the bank or building society deal with foreign currency or your British Telecom shares?

The answers to these sorts of questions are usually to be found in the City. It is called a wholesale centre because it is where the *aggregated* deposits and loans of millions of individuals and businesses are put to work. They are either traded within the financial sector itself or lent to very large customers indeed. Such 'customers' would include not just giant corporations, but the UK and foreign governments as well.

Forces of gravity

The second essential point about the City is that it is the centre of more financial markets than just that for deposits and loans. Historically speaking, the business of making deposits and loans became more sophisticated, and although the City's function as a wholesale market for funds is as vibrant as ever, there are now several ways of borrowing and investing money which have nothing (directly) to do with deposits and loans. We would mention here such markets as those for:

- **stocks and shares**
- **bonds**
- **foreign exchange**
- various forms of what the City calls **commercial paper**
- **derivatives**

and so on.

It doesn't matter if you don't understand the workings of these things! They all undergo constant change, and as already noted, nobody expects you to know before you start anyway. The point is that the City's position as a wholesale financial centre has naturally pulled a great many other financial activities into its orbit, and the bigger the City gets the more it pulls in. The City contains more foreign banks than any other financial centre, including more American banks than New York. Well over a third of the planet's foreign exchange business now passes through the City, that is, around 500 billion dollars' worth *per day*! And so it goes on, in bonds, derivatives and share dealings too.

Outdoing computers

A surprising aspect of the City's recent development has been its physical closeness in the face of better and faster communications. Why would a large bank set up a dealing room in some of the world's most expensive commercial property, when it would be so much cheaper (not to mention more pleasant) in other areas in Britain, or even abroad? Why not set up in the Lake District, the Alps, or on a Mediterranean beach? The telephone, computers and satellites work just as well in such places, don't they?

So they do, but the City is still there! The primary reason is remarkably old-fashioned. It seems that you can have as many computers and telephones as you like, but there is nothing like doing business face-to-face, or doing it with people you know. Whether that's a heartening side of human nature or a sign of its lack of imagination is for you to judge. Another reason is that employers go where the expertise is, and the more employers the more expertise – like a great big snowball rolling along.

DECIDING FROM THE START

Getting into the City, like climbing a mountain, requires more than willpower. It requires a decision on a route and sticking to that decision. If you think that you can make up a route as you go along, or if you keep changing your mind, you will either get lost or be forced to start all over again.

Multiplying the possibilities

The opportunity available in the City can also be a problem. You may find yourself interviewing for one kind of job and becoming interested in quite another, one you'd never thought of before. It's a no-win position:

- You lose enthusiasm for your original target, and make it less likely that you'll reach it.

- It makes you look indecisive and may prevent you getting an opportunity to try for a different role, at least with that particular institution.

Avoid this situation! Get it all straight right from the beginning. It is perfectly normal to change your job somewhat once you are in the City, but this is not the same thing as chopping and changing before you even get there.

Four basic roles

There are so many different sorts of jobs on offer in the City that any basic summary is bound to be incomplete. That said, it makes sense to orient yourself down one of the following paths. Changing your mind *within* one of these basic roles is much less serious than changing your mind *between* them.

1. Sales and trading

These jobs are centred on the dealing room and on the day-to-day operations of the financial markets. Sales (sometimes called **marketing**) is mainly about trading with or on behalf of customers (including retail banks) in the markets, and trading usually means actually 'making' markets and taking risk positions in them. There is considerable mobility between sales and trading jobs. The accent is on *speed* of decision-making and a certain calm under fire.

2. Corporate finance

This function is a bit of a misnomer as it involves more than just corporations. It is not usually concerned with the day-to-day operations of financial markets, but with the financing of mergers, acquisitions, and large projects (such as Eurotunnel), advising on all of the above and the syndication of loans too big to be made by a single bank. Corporate finance people are required to be able to grasp *detail*, whether it be in legal documents, financial accounts, or the workings of financial markets. The arts of negotiation and diplomacy are valuable.

3. Being an expert

Nobody actually uses this category because it's nice to think that everybody's an expert, one way or another. However, there needs to be a category for those who have a specialist skill that enables them to back up the 'front-line' activities of City institutions. This includes legal teams, economics departments, and what are usually called 'R&D' sections. This latter – research and development – usually refers to computer modelling for the benefit of trading or risk management. If you wish to find employment in this category of job you will normally need the appropriate qualifications or experience.

4. Support

Someone, somewhere, needs to process and administer the daily business of each City organisation. It's all very well for a trader to shout down a telephone and buy or sell this or that, but without a formidable support operation nothing would actually happen. There is often a distinction made between **front office** (people doing the three sorts of job above), **middle office**, and **back office**. The last two are both support roles, but the middle office tends to be directly involved with the dealing room (writing tickets, monitoring positions), and the back office with formal documentation and the management of payments and receipts arising from front office activity.

If you know which of the above appeals to you most, take a fresh look at the City. That meaningless jumble of unfamiliar names can now be sorted into four groups:

- Those that concentrate on sales and trading (*eg* the various exchanges).

- Those that concentrate on corporate finance (*eg* certain merchant banks).

- Those that concentrate on some dedicated expertise (*eg* research companies).

- Those that do a bit of everything.

Each of the above requires support staff and it is not unusual to find support staff making their way into front office jobs. Indeed, the City is proud of its star traders, managers and corporate finance gurus who started off in back office.

Qualifying for the post

A big difference between the City bank and the High Street bank is in the flexibility of the former with regard to qualifications. Of the four basic roles described in the preceding section, only one – being an expert – involved talk of being qualified. In the other three roles you will find people with postgraduate qualifications, people with a couple of A-levels, sometimes people with very little in the way of academic attainment *at all*. While the application process will *always* give a graduate a headstart over someone with A-levels, and someone with A-levels over someone with GCSEs, *nothing is impossible if you are determined enough.*

That said, it pays to be intelligent about what you have to show for yourself. There is a good rule which you ought to keep in mind first and foremost, especially if your academic qualifications aren't exactly sensational: Get in the bus before you start pushing. You may have all the drive, intelligence, and enthusiasm to progress a long way in the City, but if this isn't spotted at interview and you are offered something less than a place on a sales and trading training programme, don't rush to turn it down. It is considerably easier to get yourself into the job you want from inside a City organisation than from outside it. You may still have to be pushy, but at least you'll know who to push and when.

Being disqualified by gender

There is no particular difficulty in a woman becoming a trader or a salesperson as opposed to an expert of some sort. This may well run contrary to your received impression of City dealing rooms. Trading in particular is often portrayed as macho, and much of its language is that of warfare and other manly diversions. Don't let it fool you! Managers are increasingly aware that the complexity of modern trading calls for calm and objective traders. Overblown egos who make every decision a matter of personal virility are fast disappearing from the scene.

QUESTIONS AND ANSWERS

If I can get into a high-flying City job without a degree, why not get stuck in at 16 and forget all about college and university?

There are two good reasons why not, assuming that you have the choice. The first is that you will find your path considerably smoother if you have a degree, and even with five years' experience of administrative-type work behind you, you won't necessarily prevail over a raw graduate. Secondly, you may discover after a couple of years that you should change employer, or leave the City altogether. Do you think that your mobility will be as good without a degree as it would be with one?

Isn't it a bit unreasonable for an employer to want to know exactly what job I want when I'm new to the whole game?

If it were true, it would be most unreasonable. But City employers don't expect people without job or City experience to know exactly where in the building they want to sit. What they do appreciate, however, are signs that you have an idea of the basic direction you would like to take. It isn't the same thing at all! It shows that you have at least thought about what you are doing. If your prospective employer comes to think that you may be suited for some other role, you will be invited to consider it. No problem there, and no bad reflection on you, but 'I don't really know' sounds feeble.

Should my approach to the City be different from that of a graduate, say, if I am coming from another career?

In the essentials, it should not. You should still think about what sort of thing you'd like to do, and you should still expect to go through the same interview proccss as anybody else. As discussed in Chapter 2, your experience will be of potential interest, but only if you handle it carefully. The first thing a City employer will want to know is whether your current career has closed your mind down in any respect. Crank up the enthusiasm, but don't look childish.

SORTING OUT BANKS

The largest City employers – the banks – normally fall into the category of doing 'a bit of everything', and therefore are attractive targets for job-seekers. The problem with banks is that there are a great many of them in the City – around 500 – and it's not obvious where you should apply. Sending off 500 applications is going to be a great waste of time.

Breaking down barriers

You may have noticed that this chapter hasn't had a lot to say about building societies. The reason is that whatever the differences between banks and building societies down your High Street, they all vanish in the City. They do the same things once they're in the Square Mile, and thus when the City talks about banks, it usually includes building societies too.

There's another distinction that may apply to the High Street but doesn't in the City. Your nationality hasn't got a lot to do with whether and where you get hired. Most of the City's workforce, as you might expect, is British, but only a minority of the banks can claim to be British companies. The City is genuinely cosmopolitan and you will find Americans working in Japanese banks, British working in Arab banks and Greeks in French ones. It's all mixed up! If you happen to be Canadian and you wave your passport at the personnel people in Bank of Montreal they are most likely to say, 'So what?'

Putting banks in boxes

Just because the differences between banks in the City aren't what they are in the High Street, it doesn't mean that there aren't any differences at all. They may be divided into two camps, although you shouldn't get carried away with putting them all in neat boxes. Some banks defy simple definitions.

1. Commercial banks
These are numerically the most numerous. They have a retail network
(*ie* they have branches in high streets), although this network need
not have anything to do with the UK. They pride themselves on their
size, the enormous range of their activities and their stability.
Examples would include the British big four, Bank of America, Credit
Lyonnais, Deutsche Bank, Bank of Tokyo-Mitsubishi.

2. Investment banks
These are called merchant banks if they are British. These banks centre their activities on financial markets, and if they have any branch
network at all the purpose is to attract private investors into these
same markets. The most well known investment banks are American
– Merrill Lynch, Salomon Brothers, Goldman Sachs, for instance –
but there are plenty of non-American ones as well. Many of the
British merchant banks have been purchased by commercial banks,
but they retain a considerable degree of autonomy, including who
they hire. They *all* like to emphasise their flexibility and dynamism.

Generalising by nationality
Your nationality doesn't make a lot of difference to whether you'll
be hired by one bank rather than another, but what about the nationality of the banks you target? It might do. From Figure 10 you can
get some idea of the balance between the various foreign banks on
offer. There are a great many generalisations current in the City about
the national characteristics of different banks, and most of them
aren't worth the time of day. You would do better to keep a few
down-to-earth remarks in mind, and ignore comments of the
'Japanese banks will never promote a Brit' variety altogether.

• If you are ambitious of crowning your City career in a position of
  senior management, and in a bank of a different nationality than
  your own, you should also be ambitious of speaking the appropriate language and absorbing a different culture. It's only fair!

• The banks most likely to ignore formal qualifications, *once you're
  in*, tend to be American.

• British and American banks will probably give you more comprehensive training than the rest, although this may have as much to
  do with size as with nationality.

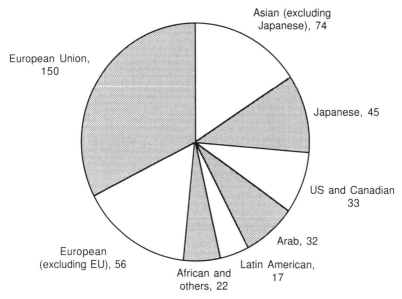

Source: *The Banker* magazine, November 1997

Fig. 10. Foreign banks in the City, 1997.

Sizing banks up

There may be a lot of banks, but they're not all big ones. While it's not always true that the largest employers offer the most opportunities, there's no doubt that a substantial staff gives you the reassurance that the bank concerned is really committed to its City operations.

UK banks in the City need not concern us here, since their general commitment to their own domestic centre should be taken as read. As for the 429 foreign banks shown in Figure 10, 40-odd have more than 300 employees, and 14 more than 1,080. The two largest – Deutsche Bank and Citibank – employed almost 6,000 people as of the survey date. (Source: *The Banker* magazine, November 1997.)

Coming up with a wish-list

Given all the above, it would be most unwise to say, 'It's got to be sales and trading at a French commercial bank' or something similarly restrictive. While the central message remains that you are advised to be reasonably focused on the sort of job you want to do and the sort of place you'd like to do it, you can go too far in that direction. Ending up with a list of just one target bank is as daft as having a list of 500.

The following approach makes more sense:

1. Choose the basic type of job you'd prefer from the four listed in 'Deciding from the start', above.

2. Come up with an initial list of, say, half-a dozen or so banks, three or four of the same type and the rest a little bit different.

3. Make sure that your targets actually do the sorts of things that you want to work in, and find out how many people they employ.

4. Make your approach as described in Chapter 6.

CRACKING THE STOCK MARKET

The stock market is not the centre around which the City revolves. It doesn't employ the most people and it doesn't provide the most lucrative business. Nevertheless, it is the largest stock market in Europe, trading as much as all the others put together, and is the world's largest market for international shares.

Furthermore, the stock market symbolises the City more than any other activity. If the evening news on television is going to mention the City at all, you can bet that it will be the stock market that gets the attention. And where do well-to-do City people live, if not in the stockbroker belt?

Burying the past

Like so much in banking and finance, the stock market is not what it was. Bowler-hatted ex-public schoolboys who talk in terms of 'a jolly good show' are about as rare as wolves in Scotland. There isn't a stock exchange floor where people wave their arms around and shout, either. That sort of thing belongs in **LIFFE** (see below). Share dealing is done these days over the telephone, and with the aid of batteries of computer screens arrayed in modern dealing rooms. In that respect, it looks very much like foreign exchange or derivatives trading.

A stock exchange floor does exist. Tourists still turn up at the 26-storey stock exchange building near the Bank of England hoping to see it. Unfortunately, the floor was obsolete as soon as it was finished, and it was never used for its intended purpose. Another enduring impression of the stock market is the division between 'jobbers' and 'brokers', a division swept away in the 1980s. Stockbrokers these days trade shares, government securities and derivatives for their own books as well as on behalf of customers.

Asking the parents

Almost all UK stockbroking firms are owned by larger companies (they may also be merchant banks, but as we have seen, the same point applies). Their names reflect this reality. Take three prominent examples:

- Barclays de Zoete Wedd (or simply BZW)
- UBS Phillips & Drew
- SBC Warburg Dillon Read.

Who, then, should you approach? The ultimate parent, or the stockbroking entity? It's a good question, but the answer is straightforward. *Go for the latter.* Stockbroking firms, especially where they also happen to be British merchant banks, are generally left alone to do their own thing. This includes hiring and firing. From your point of view – that of someone simply trying to get into the stock market – the ultimate parent of your target company is of merely academic interest. An independent firm like Cazenove & Co will look much the same to you – and train you just as well – as BZW.

Overlooking the foreigners

Don't forget that the London Stock Exchange has a great many non-UK members! You will find that share dealing in the City is important to investment banks from overseas too. American and Japanese investment banks in particular are major employers for their stock market business, among them the following:

- Lehman Brothers
- Salomon Brothers
- Merrill Lynch
- Nomura International
- Nikko Securities.

RISKING THE EXCHANGES

The **exchanges** are by far the most colourful parts of the City, both physically and in terms of the characters that work in them. The phrase 'living off your wits' means more in the exchanges than anywhere else. If you're looking for the ultimate rags-to-riches stories in banking and finance, you'll find them here, and there is probably nowhere in the City where educational qualifications matter less.

'Exchanges' here doesn't mean the stock exchange. It means financial markets where prices and volumes of business are determined by **open outcry**. Open outcry is trading in the open by authorised individuals (acting for themselves or for clients), in a specific physical location. This used to be the method of dealing on the stock exchange, of course, but share trading is now done differently.

Open outcry – in practice a noisy, physical way of doing business – may look archaic when everyone could use telephones from the comfort of their own offices. But for particular *standardised* financial products it happens to work extremely well. Where markets can move very rapidly indeed, and where players in these markets take big risks on a second's notice, it seems that you can't beat people in bright jackets shouting and waving their arms around to get business done.

Trafficking in uncertainty

LIFFE (the **London International Financial Futures and Options Exchange**, pronounced 'life') is undoubtedly the king of the London exchanges. Financial 'derivatives' have enjoyed spectacular growth over the last 15 years, and exchange-traded futures and options have mirrored this growth. LIFFE is easily the largest exchange of its kind in Europe and is a serious pretender to the world title.

It's not all LIFFE, although it's where we shall concentrate. The City also boasts the London Metal Exchange (LME), which trades half of the world's metals futures, the International Petroleum Exchange (IPE) and the London Commodity Exchange (LCE). The LME, IPE, and LCE are somewhat different from LIFFE since they trade commodity derivatives rather than financial ones, but the essential method of doing business is the same.

For the purposes of this summary, it doesn't really matter what financial futures, options or derivatives in general are all about. Suffice to say that they are inventions that allow institutions and individuals to manage and/or take risk, in a convenient form. Such risk in the case of LIFFE might be the risk of interest rates changing or of stock markets moving at some point in the future; in the case of the other three exchanges, it would be that some commodity changes price, also in the future.

Finding out more

If you wish to find out more about how exchange-traded futures and options work, especially financial ones, there are dozens of forbidding textbooks on the subject in every serious bookshop. Alternatively, LIFFE itself produces a highly-readable summary, available from its own shop (see Useful Addresses).

Working on LIFFE

There are three ways you can work on LIFFE:

- for a member of the exchange
- as a **local**
- as part of the exchange's own staff.

Working for a member of LIFFE

LIFFE is owned by around 200 members, and only these members – as companies or individuals – may trade directly on the floor. These members are usually brokers, that is to say they earn commission from clients – large banks, typically – who place orders through them. A successful broker is one who is capable of executing orders rapidly and at good prices. Their staff may be on the floor, doing the physical trading, on telephone links to their clients, or they may be involved in processing the trades.

   LIFFE produces a list of its members, and you would apply to members directly rather than via LIFFE itself.

Working as a local

There is nothing to stop you trading your own capital on LIFFE, providing of course that you fill the requirements and follow the rules of the exchange. You need to trade through a broker, and you need to negotiate the commission you will pay to both them and to whoever 'clears' your trades all by yourself. You also need to put up 'margin', *ie your own capital*, up front. It isn't cheap, and you should be warned that while some locals do become wealthy individuals, *very few* newcomers get that far and they have to say goodbye to their investment.

Working for the exchange

LIFFE employs staff to develop new business, to regulate trading and to run its systems. A booklet available from the LIFFE shop contains more detail on this work and on hiring procedures.

SUMMARY

1. The City is one of the hubs of the world's financial system, and in some respects is the most important.

2. Employers are more impressed by potential than by a detailed working knowledge of every institution and financial instrument.

3. If you want to work in the City, don't apply for something else in the belief that it will be an easy way in. Apply to where you want to work!

4. Four basic roles cover most City jobs: sales and trading, corporate finance, being an expert and support. Sort out which one is for you from the start.

5. If your academic qualifications aren't too hot, take what you're offered at your target employer and work on getting what you want once you're in.

6. Banks are by far the largest City employers.

7. Applying to banks requires you to cut down on the possibles. Three ways that you can sort them are by type (commercial/ investment), nationality and presence.

8. Even though most UK stockbroking firms are owned by larger companies, you should still apply to them directly.

9. Stockbroking firms are not all British! Don't overlook foreign investment banks.

10. LIFFE's members employ thousands of people, from PhDs to academic dropouts, but none of them is dull-witted.

CASE STUDIES

Tim takes a day off

Tim doesn't want to send in an application form without seeing where it's going. Although he lives in the same town, he has never looked around the City and doesn't even know where the Bank of England is. He takes a day's holiday and decides not only to look at the Bank but to find what else there is to see. Like a tourist, he arms himself with a guidebook. He looks at the Bank and the Lloyds' building, marvels at the concentration of office space, and he is fascinated by the brightly-coloured jackets of LIFFE traders filling the pubs around Cannon Street at lunchtime. What LIFFE is he has no idea, because the book doesn't explain. A boy in an orange jacket, about his own age, and a young man in a blue-and-white striped one walk by. They are in deep conversation. Tim doesn't care what they are saying. It's the accent! *His* accent.

Alison has a chat

Alison has got the personnel bug, and feels that a career that will involve her directly with the daily lives of a great many people is what she'd love to do. It seems to her that High Street banks would be ideal employers, because they all claim to take the needs of their staff most seriously, but the City has been nagging away in her brain. She wants to know what it's like to work there, if only to satisfy herself that she's not missing out. She'd rather not travel down to London, so she asks her own tutors if they know of any ex-student who went on to the City. Tutors ask tutors, and days later Alison has a name that she recognises. It's that of a woman who headed up the university rowing club in Alison's first year. Two telephone conversations later, Alison feels that she does not need to know a lot more. For her there just *isn't* any work that can be that interesting at 7 on a winter morning.

Roger thinks big

The local offices on Roger's list turn out to be not at all what he was thinking of. He can't help feeling that to be one step behind the real action will make him no less frustrated than he is with the Council. He goes back to the dozens of crossed-out names on his original list. If it's the stock market that interests him, he now reasons, he has to go where the stock market is. London, in other words. The problem of the family can wait, because for all he knows it's all out of the question anyway. He selects a handful of fund managers and three British stockbrokers, all in the City.

PREPARING FOR INTERVIEW

1. Do you think it would be worth swotting up on the dozens of activities involved in the City before you approach an employer? Who would be impressed by your recital of a textbook?

2. Would you be surprised to find a Japanese manager in a British stockbroking firm? Why?

3. How long do you think the average trading career is, either on an exchange like LIFFE or in the dealing room of a large bank? How long do you think you could do it? Does this make the rewards more understandable?

6
Making the Applications

LOOKING FOR VACANCIES

Banking and finance careers don't come looking for you – it's for *you* to look for *them*. If this much is obvious, you have an advantage already! For there are a lot of people out there who confine their researches to a cursory glance at the newspaper job columns over a cup of coffee and who go on to declare that 'there's nothing going'.

Looking is active

Consider the ways in which a financial organisation might recruit new employees:

1. By advertising vacancies in the press (general or specialist).

2. By notifying recruitment consultants ('head-hunters').

3. By holding a formal periodic recruiting round.

4. By choosing to interview applicants who have approached them.

There's no hard-and-fast rule about which type of organisation does what, whether in the City or High Street. Some do one or two of the above, some do a bit of each option. If you're serious about getting a job, therefore, five minutes with the newspaper is hardly enough.

Scouring the papers
There's nothing wrong with newspapers as part – and only a part – of your general search. You needn't go to the expense of buying every quality paper every day and ordering a dozen weekly financial magazines. Public or university libraries have most of what you are likely to need, and the bigger the library the more there is likely to be.

There is a lot of press to choose from, but the following are particularly recommended:

- *The Financial Times* (especially Wednesday for City appointments)
- *The Sunday Times*
- *The Sunday Telegraph.*

You are not necessarily looking for an advertisement that specifically asks for applications from people such as yourself (although if you see them it's all to the good). As pointed out in Chapter 4, a bank or any other financial institution may betray a need for people in general by an advertisement asking for someone in particular. Use your head! If an advertisement reads 'Wanted, head of department', and goes on to say that the department is a new one or is to be set up, there may well be lesser posts that need to be filled in due course. Several advertisements from the same employer may signal a general expansion, and so on. As with so much about getting a job, there is nothing wrong with being quick off the mark.

Specialist publications
As far as the specialist press is concerned, the effort of finding these periodicals isn't worth it. In any case, the cost of buying most of them – if you can't find them in a library – is prohibitive. Financial organisations that place advertisements in them are *always* looking for experienced personnel, not beginners. The big exceptions to this rule are the free newspapers and magazines available in central London in particular and often on display outside underground stations.

Local press
Finally, don't neglect your local press. High Street banks and building societies use it extensively.

Using your contacts
It could be that you know somebody already working where you would like to be. This piece of good fortune should not be dismissed out of hand. While they may not be senior enough to help you directly, they will almost certainly be able to help you in three *indirect* ways.

- They can easily find out whether their own employer is looking for people at all.

- They can get you the precise name and address for your letter.

- They may know of similar employers who are hiring.

While most people are naturally embarrassed by outright requests to 'put a good word in for me', they rarely object to giving you helpful information or advice. You should leave it up to them to give you direct help – say by securing you an interview, in the best case – and you should avoid begging for it.

Seeing the head-hunters

Head-hunters prefer to be called 'recruitment consultants', or even 'executive search agencies', but those names are a bit of a mouthful and aren't used except in polite conversation. The common link between head-hunters is that they take on part of the recruitment process for firms who pay them fees for doing so. The firms who use head-hunters are either ill-equipped to short-list candidates themselves, or they may wish to preserve a certain anonymity.

There are head-hunters who specialise in filling posts that require some experience in the appropriate field, and those that will try to 'place' those who have no experience at all. Look up 'Employment agencies' in your telephone directory. They interview prospects as if for the real thing, and may or may not decide to put them forward for actual posts.

It's not an easy option, however. Even this second category of head-hunters is unlikely to take an interest in you unless you can make it worth their while. If you have no outstanding academic record or immediately interesting skills they are most unlikely to put their credibility on the line by proposing you.

Getting in on the round

Graduates and undergraduates will have heard of the **milk round**, a recruiting system in which large companies (not necessarily involved in banking and finance) make presentations at universities. Interested students are invited to take part in an annual recruiting round and the whole process, successful or not, can be very smooth.

If you're not a university student, or you are but you missed out on the milk round, all is not lost. Far from it. You simply need to contact your target employer and ask for application forms and the date by which they should be submitted. Nobody will penalise you for having missed a presentation, and if the employer requires qualifications you don't have, they'll let you know. For regional or local hiring rounds effected by High Street banks and building societies, the same message applies. Ask for an application form and send it in time for the next available round.

Trying your luck

Writing to a list of potential employers without knowing whether they need to take anybody on has two principal drawbacks:

- You will get a lot of discouraging answers, if you get answers at all.

- You may not know to whom you should send your letter and it could well end up in somebody's bin.

Against these drawbacks, it should be said that the method can work *if it is well-directed*. This is not at all the same thing as 'blitzing the market' (below). It means that you do a little research on your target employers to find out, if possible, whether they employ people like you at all. You should also find out as best you can where your letters ought to be sent. A general or headquarters address is not necessarily appropriate.

There is a chance – a very slim chance – that your enquiry may result in you being hired even though the organisation concerned wasn't actually thinking of hiring anyone when you wrote. It happens.

SENDING OFF LETTERS

Whether you are enclosing an application form or merely trying your luck, your letters should be composed with care and attention. If a letter is well-written, it is hardly likely that it will secure you a job or an interview all on its own, but if it's badly-written it will almost certainly exclude you from consideration. 'Badly-written' covers a multitude of sins:

- Getting the name of the company or organisation wrong.

- Spelling mistakes. Don't be lazy – use a dictionary!

- Grammatical errors, including punctuation. The apostrophe 's' is frequently misused, and that looks horrible.

- Sloppy handwriting. Nobody minds handwriting – it can make a welcome change from typed script – but if you use it ensure that it is neat and clearly legible.

Remember that you are trying to join a profession. Be professional.

Sticking to the point

You could be responding to an advertisement, you could be enclosing your CV, you could be merely asking for information or you could be asking on your own initiative if you might be considered for an interview. Whichever it is, don't let yourself down.

Don't
• drivel on
• include trivial chit-chat
• labour your suitability
• use sexist language.

Do
• be courteous
• keep it businesslike
• make your 'good points' crisp and brief.

BLITZING THE MARKET

Since all the above sounds like a lot of work and bother, you may be tempted to type up a standard letter on a word-processor and 'blitz the market' with it. In other words, all you have to do is get a comprehensive list of addresses (from one of the reference works mentioned in Further Reading at the end of this book, for example) and pop your standard letter and perhaps a CV to boot into dozens of envelopes. All sorts of banks, building societies and other financial organisations all in one go. No selecting required! What could be simpler?

It's simple, all right. And lazy. And ineffective!

• Even if you send out 100 letters, there are many more financial employers in the UK than that. How do you know that you're not missing the most promising ones?

• Most personnel professionals can spot a standard letter a mile off. And they are not afraid to put things in the bin.

It's a career you're after, so get out of your chair! Spend a week or two carefully defining your targets and then approaching them with individually-written letters.

USING THE CV

Nobody needs to tell you that the CV is a most important factor in your attempt to secure a job. It is true that some employers will not require you to produce one, since they rely on their own application forms. But even application forms leave room for discretion, and what you put down requires just as much attention as your CV.

Think of the CV as your personal shop window. A well, thought out window display will always attract customers and a rough-and-ready one will deter them. Note that nobody is saying anything about the quality of what lies *behind* the window! You may be the most impressive candidate ever presented to the world of finance, but how are employers supposed to know it if they're not tempted to look at you? There are excellent guides on writing CVs in the bookshops and libraries (and see Further Reading). Even if you consider yourself a CV expert, it's not going to hurt you to check that you're giving yourself the best of chances.

Considering it's finance

A CV designed to get you an interview for a job in finance need not be very different from what you would use for a different profession. As seen in Chapter 2, there is no need for you to play up your abilities in maths or to claim that you spend your free time reading the *Bank of England Quarterly Bulletin*. If anything, these sorts of things are counterproductive. Employers in both the High Street and the City are attracted by the same sorts of people that you are, funnily enough. Demonstrating by your hobbies and interests that you are friendly and outgoing will do a lot more for you than a misguided effort to make your CV look more 'financial'.

Throwing it in for luck

Your CV is a piece of ammunition that you should think carefully about using up all at once. If you are approaching a number of employers that you have selected carefully but who have not made it known whether they might be taking people on, enclosing a CV with a preliminary letter is not necessarily a good idea. In these cases it is as well to *ask* whether you might send a CV before you actually do so:

- If you receive a reply inviting you to send your CV in, you know that there's 'something in the air'. Nobody wants CVs cluttering up their offices unless they're about to hire someone.

- If you send a CV in without being asked for it, and receive a reply to the effect that you are not required, you won't know whether it's because *nobody* is required or because there's something about *you*: your CV, your qualifications, whatever. This matters because if it's the latter case you may be able to modify your approach to other employers.

- It doesn't say much for your discretion and general professionalism if you are content to fling your personal details about like confetti. A CV should not come in with the junk mail.

FOLLOWING UP

Unfortunately not all personnel offices are as efficient as they might be, and it is not unknown for letters from potential job applicants to remain unanswered. If you send a letter out, it is reasonable to expect a reply within a week or two, even if the reply is only an acknowledgement or a note stating that your letter has been forwarded to another department.

What if nothing happens?
Don't assume that a lack of response means that nobody is interested in you! Banks and other financial organisations don't economise on postage. Most send thousands of letters out every day. If there's no reply to a letter, something has probably gone wrong somewhere. Nobody will think the worse of you if you make further enquiries, but be careful about it.

Check the address you used, and try again, keeping the tone courteous (it could be that a positive reply is on its way to you and you don't want to ruin it). Refer the intended reader to your earlier communication and ask if it has been received. If there's *still* nothing after that then you should find another – or more specific – address.

SUMMARY

1. Looking for a job in banking and finance *always* requires more than a quick look at the 'situations vacant' section of your newspaper.

2. Financial organisations recruit in different ways. Don't assume that advertising is the only one.

3. If an employer *is* using the press to advertise vacancies, it won't necessarily use every newspaper. Check several, and often.

4. Take the greatest care in writing letters to potential employers – even if it's only a request for further information.

5. Sending out standard letters to dozens of employers saying how much you want to work for them doesn't work.

6. You don't need to make your CV look particularly 'financial'. Make it *interesting*.

7. Unless a CV is specifically requested, consider holding it back on a first communication.

8. You should expect a reply to every letter or application you send out. If you don't get one, it's probably a slip-up somewhere and you should make further enquiries.

CASE STUDIES

Tim focuses on LIFFE

When the Bank of England information arrives, Tim can see almost immediately that he is just not in the academic league required. His pass in maths isn't up to standard, and though he could really work for a retake through evening classes, he can't see that the effort would be worth it. This leaves him free in his mind to concentrate on LIFFE. He sends off for information from LIFFE, and in due course orders two brochures from the LIFFE shop. When he feels that he understands something of futures and options – creatures he didn't think existed barely a week before – he asks the exchange for a list of its members. He writes off to several, asking if they have any possible vacancies for trainees. After three discouraging replies, Tim receives an invitation to send in a CV. He writes it out by hand, and stays late at work to put it on the word processor. There is a CV-writing package in the computer software, and although he sticks to his own format he uses it to check that he's left nothing off.

Alison adds two for luck

The High Street bank that attracted Alison in the first place gets her first application. She fills in the form that she's had since the presentation, specifically mentioning her interest in personnel management. There aren't any 'trick' questions, but it's thorough and she takes her time over it. That one sent off, she thinks that she had better hedge her bets a bit, so she goes down to the careers library and writes off to one further bank – an ex-building society – and a High Street building society, asking for careers information and application forms.

Roger reads the papers

It is now part of Roger's routine to drop by the library twice a week to scan the job advertisements in the newspapers. He isn't expecting to find an advertisement asking for someone like him, but he reasons that he might get an idea of who is hiring in general. In the meantime, he sends in his letters to the stockbrokers and the fund managers that he has selected. Two of the latter write back almost immediately, explaining that they are not looking to expand for the present. A little later, a stockbroker asks him if he'd care to send in his CV.

PREPARING FOR INTERVIEW

1. What is your reaction when you receive a letter that starts 'Dear Sir' if you are female, or 'Dear Madam' if you are male? Does it make you less likely to read the contents, or don't you care? Why would a personnel officer feel any differently?

2. What sort of letter would you think was appropriate if a potential employer were to reply to you? A chatty and effusive one, or something rather more businesslike? Does that tell you how *you* should approach *them*?

3. Would you ever include a photograph of yourself with a CV if not specifically asked for it? If you would, how do you think that it might help you?

7
Interviewing with Attitude

FORGETTING ABOUT SCHOOL

An invitation to attend an interview changes your attitude to the business in hand. So far, your approach to financial organisations has – quite frankly – focused on presenting your past achievements in the best possible light. As soon as you are invited to interview, however, what you have done in the past fades to a secondary importance.

An interview is not simply an opportunity for you to repeat what you may have already noted on your CV or application form. Of course, it is perfectly normal to be asked to comment on some of the things you have done, but you should not lose sight of the fact that the primary importance of the interview is for an employer to assess whether you can achieve things in the *future*.

Go to an interview with the attitude that you must try to project your abilities and your personal qualities as they are *now*. You will do much better than if you keep reminding your interviewer how great you were at school. That may have got you the interview, but it's done its work.

DRESSING THE PART

Interviews for careers in banking and finance are not necessarily different from those for any other sort of career, and neither is getting dressed up for them. You should dress smartly and conservatively, like the employees you see in every bank or building society in the land, and your personal hygiene should be irreproachable.

The common-sense rules

Don't
- dress up like a Victorian dandy or a duchess at the races
- dress down as if you are Richard Branson or a Spice Girl

- 'make a statement' about your political beliefs.
- clutter yourself with ostentatious jewellery or perfumes.

Do
- clean your suit, iron your shirt or blouse, polish your shoes
- tidy up your hair, visiting the hairdressers' if necessary
- pay attention to your own cleanliness, to your fingernails and teeth
- think 'respectable' in place of 'flashy'.

JUDGING THE STYLE

It is unlikely that you will be required to dazzle your questioner with all you know about the financial system, although for some City posts you might be asked your views on some current market event. Even this possibility is much less threatening than it sounds.

> **An interview has got as much to do with your style as it has with your substance.**

Two sorts of question
It may help to separate interview questions into two types. Each type requires a different sort of response:

- **Substance** questions are questions about the facts, particularly *your* facts: things you wrote in your CV or application form that need expanding upon. There is no trick involved. They are simply requests for information. Give it!

- **Style** questions don't have a 'right' and a 'wrong'. They might be about your views on some item in the news or on your hopes and ambitions. They aren't tricks either! If you are asked whether you think the stock market will fall or rise, for instance, *it doesn't matter what your view actually is*. The point of this sort of question is to see how you express yourself, not what you express.

Being able to spot a style question as it comes up is most useful. A lot of banking and finance is about talking to people: explaining to them, persuading them. Don't worry about whether your questioner agrees with you that taxes will go up or whatever. If you do, you're missing the point. Your reply to a style question is being noted not so much for its content as the way you put it. This means using eye-to-eye contact, the appropriate body language and stringing together coherent sentences. If you get a style question, remind yourself that the real question lies behind it and is always the same: *Can we trust this candidate to talk to our customers and clients?*

Putting on a style

What sort of style, then, will impress a bank? Should you put on one style for a City stockbroker and another for a building society? What style do financial institutions like to see? There are two rules which apply to all of these concerns: a negative one and a positive one.

1. Don't put on an assumed personality in an interview. Unless you are currently employed by the Royal Shakespeare Company, you'll come across as false. The interviewer may not know exactly what it is, but he or she will know that something 'isn't right'.

2. Recall what was said in Chapter 6 about writing letters: you are trying to join a profession. Keep your own style. But speak and act in a *professional* manner. Keep your dignity, stay courteous and calm. Like professionals in all walks of life.

PUSHING THE TRUTH

There are plenty of things about you that an interviewer isn't going to check. And there are plenty of things that *can't* be checked, even if the interviewer wanted to. While you most certainly draw the line against telling an outright lie, might you just push the truth a tiny bit to help yourself along?

Staying on track

Let's say that you went to trial for a place in a county athletics squad, and you failed to get selected for the 1500m by a whisker. Why not say that you *were* selected, and that you competed at county level for a short time? Who is going to be bothered to find out? And you were good enough, anyway, and if you had gone to another trial you would surely have made it. . . It's not worth it. It's not that nobody's going to be bothered to find out. The biggest problem is that your interviewer may mention it to someone else, and you may have to repeat your claim, you might embellish it a little more, and either you finally come up against someone who *did* compete at the same time as you say you did, or you get the story muddled and the whole thing starts falling apart.

The truth is much easier to remember! If you think that if you get found out you can shrug it off and make a joke of it, that won't wash either. If you lie once, people will assume that you lie all the time.

REPEATING THE EXERCISE

It is difficult to generalise about the way interviews are arranged. It may be that you have one interview, or several; in the latter case, the interviews may be spread over several days or even weeks, and you may find yourself going back and forth a number of times. This is fairly common in the City, and by no means unknown with High Street employers.

Take a look at Figure 11. The message is that repeated interviews can mean good news or merely a bit of administrative inefficiency on the part of your intended employer. Getting fed up about going back and forth to say pretty much the same thing will get you nowhere. Your best course is to smile sweetly and put up with it.

KEEPING YOUR COOL

Losing your temper at an interview is just about the worst thing you can do. Fortunately, the banking and finance industry takes personnel – and therefore hiring people – very seriously. It is *most unlikely* that you will have to put up with unprofessional conduct by an interviewer, and there should be no reason to let your feelings get the better of you.

Having said that, there are two sorts of questions that you may find offensive:

- Reference to your sex, race, or any physical handicap. Harassment or discrimination on these grounds is usually illegal (see Chapter 1).

- Inquiring after your 'real' motives and ambitions.

In the first case, you have recourse to law, and you may terminate the interview without necessarily impairing your ability to get the job (assuming you still want it). In the second, you should ask yourself whether the questioner is trying to see how you behave 'under fire'. It is a legitimate – if old-fashioned – way of assessing you.

Either way, you will note that there has been no mention of storming out or anything like that. As you have seen throughout this chap-

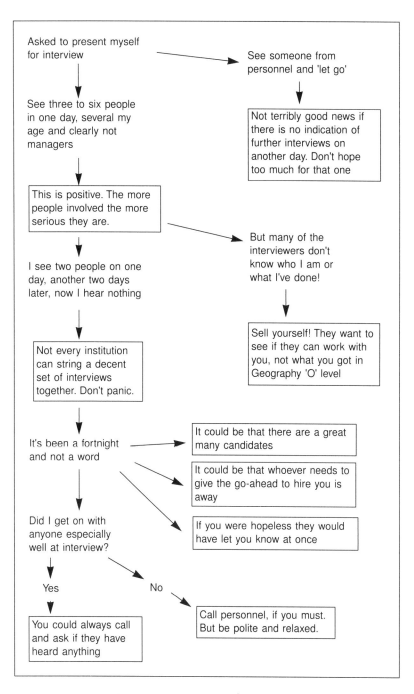

Fig. 11. Interviews – what is going on?

ter, a **professional attitude** should be maintained even in the extreme situation. If you reach the point – again, a most unlikely event – where you feel that the interview should be terminated, do it firmly, coolly and politely. Remember who you are, even if your interviewer is a worm.

SUMMARY

1. An interview is more than a verbal repetition of what is on your CV or application form. Don't keep going on about what you did at school.

2. Dress smartly and conservatively, and don't neglect your personal hygiene.

3. Interview questions may be divided into those of substance and those of style. If the question is not about a matter of fact, it is one of the latter, and it is the way you express yourself rather than what conclusion you arrive at that matters.

4. Avoid putting on a personality that you think will appeal to your prospective employer. Stick to your own.

5. Try to behave in a professional manner in every interview situation.

6. Don't lie in interview, even if your assertion can't be disproved. Don't even 'push the truth'.

7. It may be that you are recalled more than once to face repeated interviews. Even if you suspect that it's due to inefficient organisation, you'll have to put up with it.

8. Don't lose your temper, even under provocation. Even in the worst situation you gain nothing by behaving in an undignified fashion.

CASE STUDIES

Tim has no way of telling

It isn't as Tim expected. Having dressed and prepared himself meticulously, he is met at LIFFE by a young woman, who signs him into the building, dons a bright jacket and leads him directly into the noise of the trading floor. They stop beside a booth, where a couple of young men and another woman are on telephones. They shake his hand absent-mindedly and he is told to wait. After several minutes, an unshaven prop-forward of a man emerges from one of the futures pits, swears, and shakes Tim by the hand. 'Let's go out', he says.

Is it a grilling or isn't it? Tim is glad he figured out what futures are all about, anyway. After 20 minutes, feeling cold from sitting on a bench, Tim makes his way back to the underground station. 'We'll be in touch.' What does that mean?

Alison finds it worrying

If the interviews had been tough, she wouldn't have minded. She had worked herself up for that. But a series of pleasant chats and a written aptitude test leave her feeling a little bit empty. She can't help but worry that she hadn't got anything impressive across, that she hadn't made them understand that it's personnel that she'd really like to do, and the other candidates looked so well-groomed and bright! Yes, everything went smoothly, but there hadn't been anything that could have caught anyone out. She remembers that the High Street banks are famed for their recruitment procedures, and the quality of their training. Do they get the most out of recruits by making them relaxed, and chatting to them? Alison can't see how. She must have done something wrong.

Roger talks all day

The letter said 'present yourself for interview'; it didn't say how many. Roger spends 15 minutes with someone in personnel, he is shown around the dealing room, and then sat behind a desk in an office with glass walls just off it. He can see the banks of screens clearly from where he waits, and he tries to guess the ages of the people in front of them. Lots younger, but some definitely older. The interviews follow on one after the other, quarter of an hour each, head of this, head of that, traders, salespeople, research people – and two hours later he is fetched by personnel. He has said lots of the same things over and over again, he's talked about himself, the markets, what he thinks of particular stocks. When he gets outside again he feels drained.

PREPARING FOR INTERVIEW

1. Do you suffer from interview nerves? If you do, have you ever sat down to think about why this is? Do you grovel before other people? If not, why do it in an interview?

2. Irrespective of party, which politicians impress you or have impressed you? How do (or did) they perform in front of the cameras? What makes a politician good in television interviews? Can you learn anything by watching them?

3. If a potential manager showed absolutely no interest in your academic qualifications, would you find it irritating or refreshing?

8
Coping with Rejection

DWELLING ON MISTAKES

It is a wretched experience to go through the whole tense process of research, application and then interview only to be rejected at the end of it. Somehow the very politeness of the letter bringing the bad news ('we regret to say', 'wish you luck for the future', *etc*) makes it worse. It could be that you were in two minds about the employer anyway, in which case you may actually be relieved that a difficult decision has been taken out of your hands. But more often the opposite is true. Going along for interview and actually seeing where you might work can of themselves increase your desire to succeed. The disappointment can be difficult to bear, and you end up running your interviews over and over again like a film to try and see where you 'went wrong'.

Living with failure
A dispassionate look at the situation will tell you that you have no way of knowing whether your rejection has anything to do with what you did wrong or not. You don't know what outside factors were at work (what the other candidates were like, whether the employer thought that you were excellent but wouldn't fit into an existing team, for example) and you don't know whether you were an outside chance to begin with and did well to get an interview at all. You may well be dwelling on mistakes that never were!

The trouble is that being dispassionate about it is terribly difficult, especially in the first day or two. If this is the case with you, try a bit of the passionate instead!

Try thinking sport
Sport is a good analogy here because success and failure in sport are very public and very obvious. Think of a great champion, in any discipline you like, and then ask yourself *what it is* that makes or made that person a champion. Is it the fact of remaining undefeated, or of

coming back from defeat? And where is the great emotion in sport? Not losing, or being written off after failure and triumphing all the same?

We *all* fail. The most successful people you will ever met – and not just sportspeople – are not those who have never failed, but they recognise a fact of life when they see it and can move on.

APPEALING THE SENTENCE

Except in unusual circumstances, no employer is going to take you on because you come back and moan about being rejected. Apart from making a nuisance of yourself, appealing against the decision makes you look immature and hence considerably less suitable as an employee than you were to start with. So don't do it.

The 'unusual circumstances' are essentially twofold:

- Where you suspect that you have suffered some form of illegal discrimination. You would not be advised to go back to the employer, however, without taking competent advice beforehand. You may inadvertently compromise your own case.

- Where you have been told that you lack some essential qualification (say an adequate GCSE pass in maths or English), and you go out, study and get it. Of course there would be a delay of months between the 'rejection' and the 'appeal', and you may be required to start from scratch anyway.

USING THE EXPERIENCE

Moving on from a rejection letter *doesn't* mean that you shut the whole business out of your mind. Defeats often have lessons in them, and absorbing these lessons will make you stronger next time around. Why let the whole thing act as a great big negative?

The good things that you can pull out of the situation may be:

- You have gained priceless interview experience. It is one thing to practise in mock interviews and quite another to go through the real thing. The next time you go you will have a better idea of what to expect.

- You may have met or may have been interviewed by people other than personnel staff who currently work at the sort of job you want to do. Were there any hints in their way of speaking or in their dress that you could use?

- Before and during the interview process, were there any aspects of *you* that seemed to be of particular interest to your potential employer? Was there anything about you that they seemed to like and wanted to talk about? Could you not make it a bigger feature of your CV and general approach in future?

HIDING THE DISGRACE

It is difficult enough to come to grips with being turned down without having to admit it to others. In banking and finance, however, this is an unnecessary worry. Whether you have been rejected from a job in the City or in the High Street, you will find that a great many people actually working where you want to work have been through the same thing as you. Indeed, in the case of the City, it is possible that *most* employees know what being rejected is like – the author included!

In a way, this phenomenon is a sign of the basic health of banking and finance as a career. The financial world is changing so rapidly that new opportunities arise all the time, and people both inside and outside the system are forever trying to take them. And they expect to fail at least as often as they succeed.

Dealing with the failure

When it comes to making another attempt at getting a job, therefore, don't be ashamed of having failed in the past. There is *no* disgrace. If the question arises at interview or anywhere else, keep your cool.

Don't
- make a big deal of it
- be embarrassed
- hazard guesses about why you didn't succeed
- criticise or denigrate the organisation that rejected you.

Do
- be open about it
- keep your head up
- maintain a mature attitude
- acknowledge the good points of the organisation that rejected you.

You never know – you may have more in common with your interviewer than you think!

STARTING ALL OVER

When you fall off a bicycle or a horse, as the conventional wisdom
goes, you should clamber back on as quickly as you can. With a rejection letter in your hands, however, it's not such good advice. Getting
a job is too complicated, and it may not be at all obvious – and probably never will be – why you didn't make it. Hurrying to get another
application in may sound like just the thing to get over your disappointment, but you ought to make sure that there's nothing you can
improve on first. Starting all over again is best done methodically.
Cover the following:

1. Take a little break from the whole thing. A couple of days or a
   week without doing *anything* about the next step will help you
   more than just about anything.

2. Concentrate on absorbing all the *positive* experience that came out
   of last time around. Don't concentrate on what you imagine you
   did wrong, but on the things that came out of the situation that
   could improve your whole approach.

3. Question the target you chose first time around. Could it be possible that you are looking at the wrong sort of institution?

4. Take the time to choose your next target, once you have assured
   yourself that your general direction is good. Research the next possible employer at least as thoroughly as the first.

SUMMARY

1. Failing at what we try to do can be hard to live with, but it's something that happens to *anybody* that tries *anything*.

2. The most successful people aren't those who don't ever fail. They
   are those who aren't afraid to try again. And again!

3. Don't complain to the employer who rejected you, and don't ask
   for another go unless there are very special circumstances.

4. Dig into the experience you have gained and draw positive lessons from it.

5. Banking and finance is a highly fluid world, and opportunities come up all the time for those inside or outside it. A lot of people in financial employment right now know all about rejection.

6. Don't be embarrassed about having been turned down for a job if you are asked about it in a subsequent interview.

7. *Never* criticise the situation or individuals that turned you down in a subsequent interview somewhere else. It's unprofessional and, besides, you don't know who your interviewer's friends are.

8. Start again only after a short break and with a calm, methodical attitude.

CASE STUDIES

Tim is down, but not out

Tim's first reaction to the letter of rejection he receives is to shrug his shoulders, as if to say that it was all a dream anyway. But the real emotion comes later, when he's on his way to the office he loathes. What did he mess up? What didn't he know? Such a short letter, no frills. He is miserable all day, and when he gets home he goes out into the little back garden and looks at the clouds. Then he realises that he is not about to give up. The LIFFE shop surely has other books, the heavyweight stuff. He is going to get another interview and he will know more than what tourists know next time he is asked. And he will be more relaxed, too. Just as neat, but he might smile.

Alison falls at the first

At least the wait is over, but there's no denying that it's hard when it's a rejection. There are the two other interviews coming up, but her confidence is badly shaken. Successful at both sport and at her studies, she finds that she's not very good at taking losses. It's a bit embarrassing, too, because her friends keep asking if she's heard. Each time she has to confess the truth it's like being rejected afresh. She wonders whether she's going to get a job at all, a thought she's never had before, but she realises that she can't go into her other interviews depressed, so she goes back to her CV and thinks hard about what she can do well. Of course there are things anyone would be proud of. And working with people? She's *sure* of it.

Roger waits for the post

It's all bad stuff. With the exception of the stockbroker who gave him interviews, all responses to Roger's initial letters have been negative, and he has low hopes for the next wave he sends out. He can't help thinking that his interviews can't have been brilliant, either, because the silence stretches to ten days and there is no further word. Having discussed matters with his wife, he feels a move to London is possible if it all works out. If it all comes to nought now the let-down will be awful. He toys with the idea of doing an MBA, but that will not be cheap.

PREPARING FOR INTERVIEW

1. Do you admire tennis players who throw their racquets around when they lose a point? Is applauding the skill of an opponent a weakness? Name a great sporting champion who was graceless in defeat.

2. If you have been invited to interviews several times, but have not yet landed a job offer, what does that tell you? Do you think that *everybody* gets an interview? Are you too proud to ask for help on your personal presentation and speaking style?

3. If you failed an academic examination, would you want to re-sit it straight away? What is so different about applying for a job, or getting interviewed for one?

9
Striking Gold Twice

GETTING MORE THAN ONE OFFER

Getting two job offers at the same time is always a possibility if you apply to several employers at once. There is no reason, either, why you couldn't be rejected by one employer one week and offered posts with different ones the next. Having to choose between two offers is a delightful dilemma to have, especially if you've been disappointed in the past. But it is by no means unknown for the lucky 'double winners' to either take the 'wrong' choice or, worse, to mess it all up and walk away with nothing at all.

PLAYING IT STRAIGHT

Funnily enough, the best way to deal with the situation has a lot in common with coping with rejection:

- Be honest and open about it, especially with the employers concerned.

- Acting in haste or on impulse is not a good idea. You will not be expected to give a yes or no on the spot, so don't.

BURROWING INSIDE

The first step with any job offer, let alone when you have two of them, is to clear up any questions you may have about it. Your starting salary and your initial role should be made clear in the offer, but there are a whole host of details that you may not have thought to ask at interview and which might make a difference to you:

- Which office are you to work in?
- What fringe benefits are on offer?
- Who is to be your immediate manager? Have you met him or her?
- How much holiday will you be entitled to?

The offer letter may well invite you to telephone if you have further questions. This is not merely politeness. If there isn't a number indicated you should have no inhibitions about calling personnel via the main switchboard number.

Extending the deadline
Like all professions, that of banking and finance demands that you are thorough. You can hardly be criticised for being thorough with your own career, and taking the time to reach an informed decision. Having said that, unless you have a good reason for it, a request for the employer to extend the deadline by which you should respond to an offer will be considered unreasonable. The usual deadline of a week or so is normally considered more than adequate, and no employer is going to hang around while you see if you can get a better offer elsewhere.

If you have one job offer in the bag, and suspect that another is on its way but is unlikely to arrive before the deadline of the first expires, you are better advised to explain the situation to the *second* employer, who may get a move on if they think highly of you and may be prepared to confirm that good news is in the offing. Whether they do or not, the first deserves the courtesy of a yes or no within the appointed time.

Finding a neutral
A person who can give you informed and objective advice on which of two jobs is best for you is rarely on hand in this sort of situation. If you do know someone in the business already, someone *not* directly involved with your job search but who will know what each of the two employers concerned is like to work for, why not ask?

PREDICTING THE FUTURE

Don't. It's a favourite occupation of journalists and financial pundits to predict which banks and other financial institutions are on the way up and which are on the way down. You may find newspaper comment to the effect that one of the organisations that has offered you a job will or won't do well next year, or something of that sort.

Unless the report is one of fact, ignore it. If you are trying to decide between two employers, you should leave airy suppositions well alone. Think of it this way: if pundits or journalists could really predict the future, they wouldn't be working for a living, would they? A remarkable feature of the last 20 years of financial history is the speed at which banks written off have come back 'from the dead' and at which successful ones have turned to ashes, and *all* contrary to expectations.

Choosing on merit
Go for the job on its own merits, not because somebody said that one of your potential employers is going to have a difficult third quarter or whatever. Whether your employer is a future 'winner' or not is something nobody knows, and you would do well to leave it where it belongs – in the lap of the gods.

PLAYING THE AUCTIONEER

Financial institutions have money, don't they? And there are two of them who want you, right? So why not use your position of 'power' to get at least one of them to pay you more? Why not tell either or both of them that you will accept a post at the other unless the starting salary is increased?

The City in particular has a deserved reputation for paying up for the people it wants, and you may reason that trying a bit of bargaining will bring you a bit of respect even if it doesn't come off. The worst that can happen, you may reason, is that one or both employers will simply say no and you are no worse off than you were before.

Playing a pointless and dangerous game
Why it's pointless
- Starting salary is an insignificant part of a career's earnings.

- Financial organisations are keenly aware of the going rate for any given job and consider themselves fair in applying it.

- No employer is going to upset current employees by paying an inexperienced newcomer as much as they receive.

- You may be one of several new hires, and if you are all at the same level it would be most unfair to offer you more than the others.

Why it's dangerous
- Managers from different institutions often know each other, whether in the City or the High Street, and they may well compare notes.

- Without experience, you are not indispensable. While your offer is unlikely to be withdrawn, you risk the employer doing nothing at all and allowing the deadline to elapse without renewal.

- It is a bad way to start work, and respect is the last thing you will gain by the exercise. 'Too big for your boots' will cling to you and possibly blight your career from the start.

'Playing the auctioneer' only works with heavyweights – experienced individuals who have proved that they can deliver. At the beginning of your career you are most definitely a lightweight, no matter how talented.

WALKING IT OUT

Sometimes there is no material reason that leads you to favour one employer over another, or, if there is, you don't know it. If the conditions of the proposed contracts are more or less the same, and you have positive feelings about working for both, it's time to use the 'no-rush' rule.

'Walking it out' works well in a great many situations. It starts off by assuming that you are terribly close to the problem you're wrestling with. In the case of two job offers, you've probably thought of little else outside CV, interview and all the rest of it for quite some time. It might have been *weeks* since you've been to bed without thinking or worrying about getting a job. One part of you is saying, 'decide and get it over with', but the other can't actually make the decision for fear of getting it wrong!

Taking time out

Go for a walk. Do yourself a favour and take a day out, much in the same way as you are advised to do if you've been rejected. The essential part isn't the walking – it could be another pursuit altogether – but being *alone* and being *quiet*. If you've spent weeks talking, being talked to, and receiving advice, and all that hasn't helped you to decide, go to the opposite extreme. You are *too close* to the subject, so step back for a moment. It's funny the way a bit of silence helps you hear.

SUMMARY

1. Unless you have a clear preference between two job offers, use at least some of the time you are given before the offers lapse.

2. Don't hesitate to go back to an employer who has offered you a job if you have further questions, no matter how trivial you think they might sound.

3. Unless you have a very good reason to extend a deadline on acceptance of an offer, give a yes or no before the date given. It is unprofessional to ask for more time.

4. If you are lucky enough to have a source of informed and genuinely unbiased advice, ask for an opinion.

5. Don't pay attention to newspaper comment on the future success of your potential employers unless it is firmly grounded in fact.

6. As an inexperienced newcomer, you have almost no bargaining power as regards your job offer. Leave the bargaining until you have experience.

7. If you are dishonest in your dealings with your two potential employers, you run a decent risk of being caught. Managers in different financial organisations frequently know each other, in the City or the High Street alike.

8. If you cannot decide between the two offers, it is suggested that you spend a peaceful day, quite alone. It may be that you are just too close to get a decent perspective and there's simply too much 'noise' for you to think straight.

CASE STUDIES

Tim asks for advice

The elation of receiving one job offer to start as a trainee on LIFFE turns to disbelief when the second arrives. Tim's first thought is to ask more money, for although he might make a great deal in the space of a few years, the starting salary isn't any better than that he receives at present. He dismisses the notion after a few minutes, because he really wants to be there on the floor and he's not going to play dice with it. He needs advice – is there any difference between these employers and, if so, which will do him the most good? It takes some nerve, but he waits until the markets have all closed and calls LIFFE. When he is put through to the unshaven prop forward, he reminds him who he is and why he is calling. Is there any advice? 'Well done,' comes the reply. 'LIFFE entrance, 12 sharp.'

Alison doesn't wait

There is a job offer from the building society, but nothing from the bank since the interview. Alison liked both organisations very much, and it seems that she can get into personnel in both cases if she does well in her initial training. She would find it difficult to decide between them, but the deadline on the offer received is short and she knows that she should respect it. She does, and days afterwards she receives another offer. She has no regrets, but writes a polite refusal back.

One is enough for Roger

It's only one offer, but the stockbroker eventually comes through and there's a fairly detailed job offer in equity sales for Roger. He could hardly have imagined it better. After discussing with his wife the prospect of working in London, he decides that he will give commuting a try and take it from there. He accepts the offer in writing, as requested.

PREPARING FOR INTERVIEW

1. Should starting salary play any part in whether you choose one job over another? How different do you think banks and other financial organisations can really be in matters of pay? Have you asked what you might be earning three or five years down the line?

2. Are you aware that one of the largest and most profitable US commercial banks of 1997 was in such difficulties a decade ago that it was widely rumoured to be on the brink of collapse? If the management of Baring Brothers & Co couldn't spot the problems that caused that bank to collapse in early 1995, how could *you* have guessed at it?

3. Have you ever been stuck on a personal or emotional problem, only to find that a period of solitude or silence produces the solution? Have you ever noticed that mechanical problems can be resolved in the same way? Have you ever given it a go?

10
Making the Most of Success

SHARPENING UP

Once you've signed on the dotted line, relief is probably your first emotion, and possibly a quiet euphoria the second. When you look back at all the letter-writing and CV-sending and perhaps the rejections too, the temptation to celebrate is perfectly natural. No matter how lowly your foothold, you are from now on part of a most dynamic profession, and a great many opportunities will open themselves to you sooner or later.

Don't let it all go, however! Whatever you did to get yourself sharp for interview – reading the newspapers, dressing smartly, acting in a professional manner – should be continued once you embark on the real thing. As Figure 12 shows, there are plenty of challenges waiting for you from day one of your new career. The sharper you are when you start, the more you will gain:

- First impressions take a long time to erase, even among your new colleagues. You owe it to yourself to give as good an initial impression as you can.

- If you go in 'switched on', you will suffer less from first-day nerves.

- You may consider that all your interviews are over. They aren't! They won't be called interviews, but when you meet managers of varied seniority over your first few days they will be sizing you up, even if you are chatting informally.

GETTING AROUND

The first days and weeks of your new job have a characteristic that you may never have considered before. In any financial organisation, as we have seen all along, there is very little that you do on your own. Banking and finance is a service industry, and like all others it

Fig. 12. Getting the best possible start.

depends on its people and the teamwork it can generate. Hence it is far more important that you get to know the people you will work with than the machines (computers, essentially) that you will use.

In office situations it is normal that employees form circles of friends, and know their circle much better than anyone else in the building. As a new arrival you should be aware of this, and you should avoid sticking with one group of colleagues for as long as possible. When you start work, everyone in your new office will be curious about you, and will be receptive to spending a bit of time with you. *Don't waste it!*

Using your novelty value

Getting around means that you should use your novelty value to meet everybody you reasonably can, from the cleaners to employees that you would not normally come across from day to day. Don't barge around being a nuisance, but if there is an opportunity to introduce yourself, take it. What tends to happen otherwise is that you settle into work and your own group and it becomes too odd to go over to other people who you should know but don't. The more people you know, and can stop for a moment to talk with, the easier and happier you will find your early career. If you depend on office gossip to 'know' people you will do them – and yourself – a disservice.

QUALIFYING AS A PROFESSIONAL

Banking and finance treats its professional qualifications most seriously. They are not merely optional extras, nice strings of letters that you can put after your name or certificates that you can put up on your wall. In some cases you are required to pass professional examinations to make any career progress at all.

It's not strictly true that the High Street and the City each have their own exams, but the skills required of employees are somewhat different, and it would be inappropriate to require the same expertise from everybody.

Graduating in the High Street
The Chartered Institute of Bankers (CIB), which has a sister organisation called **The Chartered Institute of Bankers in Scotland**, offers a number of qualifications to bank and building society staff. A series of examinations ultimately leads to the prestigious Associateship of the CIB; a qualification, by the way, that is recognised in countries all over the world.

The various levels of qualifications are as follows:

- **Certificate in Financial Services Practice** (CFSP). This is a basic foundation designed primarily for school-leavers.

- **Banking Certificate**. This is pitched at roughly first-year degree level.

- **Associateship**. This brings with it a simultaneous BSc (Hons) in Financial Services, as agreed with the University of Manchester Institute of Science and Technology (UMIST).

- The CIB also sponsors further study for those intended to fill senior management posts.

The **graduate** intake of High Street banks and building societies is almost always expected to pass the Associateship exams within two to four years. There is nothing stopping a non-graduate from following the same route, of course, but the compulsion to do so is often self-imposed.

The structure of CIB in Scotland examinations is slightly different. The addresses of both CIB and CIB in Scotland are in Useful Addresses.

Regulating fund management and the City

City employers and fund managers are very careful to give the go-ahead to trade and to speak with clients *only* to those individuals authorised by its regulatory bodies. A great deal of money can be involved in the sorts of financial transactions they specialise in, and a simple mistake can obviously do substantial damage.

The **Financial Services Authority** regulates a wide range of financial activities, and not just in the City. It devolves supervisory powers to several **self-regulatory organisations (SROs)**. Those most likely to concern us here are:

- **The Securities and Futures Authority (SFA)** sets exams that all intending wholesale (*ie* City) traders and advisers *must* pass before they can actually do their work. SFA can also suspend or ban an individual from working in wholesale markets. Note that LIFFE and the stock exchange are governed by other SROs.

- **The Investment Management Regulatory Organisation (IMRO)** has a practically identical role to SFA in its regulation and authorisation of the fund management business. It too requires that all individuals who deal or advise pass its exams.

The exams as set by SFA and IMRO do not require years of study, as with those set by the CIB and CIB in Scotland. They are much simpler in format, and are designed to be taken after several weeks of study at home, usually at the start of your career.

ACCEPTING BAD NEWS

It's a fact of financial life that employers go through difficult times and shed staff. Even though the banking and finance profession is growing, as you may recall from Chapter 1, it doesn't mean that every organisation is growing too. Statistically, redundancy shouldn't happen to you, but it clearly happens to *somebody*.

It's not something that you should worry about, and certainly not at the start of a career. Once inside the profession, it usually takes more than mere redundancy to shake you out, assuming that you want to stay:

- Having work experience and possibly professional qualifications in *any* industry has got to be good news.

- You will be far more aware of possible openings with other employers than an outsider ever can be.

- Other employers will be aware of the situation and may contact you directly if they happen to be expanding their operations.

If redundancy strikes, it is a small consolation to reflect that banking and finance has got to be one of the best professions to be made redundant in, and *nobody* is going to think any worse of you, except perhaps yourself. Accept it and move on.

SUMMARY

1. You should prepare for your first day at work with the same thoroughness as for interview.

2. First impressions of you will take time to undo – so make them good.

3. Capitalise on your novelty value by introducing yourself to as many people as possible.

4. Your career may depend on getting professional qualifications. Don't take the attitude that exams no longer matter!

5. CIB qualifications in particular are well-regarded considerably beyond UK banks and building societies.

6. SFA and IMRO are similar bodies that regulate the City and fund managers respectively. Employees who trade or advise *must* pass the relevant exams.

7. Given that banking and finance is a healthy and dynamic industry, being made redundant is not as serious as it can be in other careers.

CASE STUDIES

Tim hits the ground running

Tim knows he's just a trainee, and that his employer could find another just like him at the drop of a hat. So he starts as he means to continue – he works. He doesn't mind that most of it is running about with pieces of paper, and he doesn't bat an eyelid when he's shouted at either. He only has to look across the floor to the locals who were pointed out to him when he arrived; a little group of them, thirtyish, respected, rich. As he constantly reminds himself, 'They all started like this.'

Roger makes a good impression

It's not hard for Roger to start off well informed, since it's been his hobby to follow shares for years, but he makes a real effort and follows the daily movements of the stock market in some depth for days beforehand. The effort pays off from his first morning, when he discovers that he can hold his own in discussing market conditions with his new colleagues. He can see that he has made a solid first impression and it helps him overcome his nervousness at meeting everybody on the dealing floor. He is further reassured by someone who tells him that fresh-faced graduates 'get on everybody's nerves.'

PREPARING FOR INTERVIEW

1. When you were new to a school or at university, did you find it easier to meet and talk with everybody in your first year than you did later on? Did you ever regret not knowing some individuals until you were about to leave? Could you have been more open?

2. Are professional qualifications a waste of time? Haven't you had enough of exams? Would you go to a doctor who didn't have professional qualifications?

3. If you were selected for a team in your favourite sport, would you be worried about being dropped in the future? If you were dropped, wouldn't your experience help you get back in?

Glossary

Back office. The settlements department of a financial institution, especially in the City.

Bank. A duly authorised financial institution that manages money and provides financial services for its customers.

Big Bang. The final stage of the 1980s stock market reforms, which abolished fixed commissions for the purchase and sale of shares and removed the distinction between brokers and traders ('jobbers'). So-called because a number of measures took effect on a single day (27 October 1986).

Big four. The four largest retail banks in the UK: HSBC Midland, Nat West, Barclays, Lloyds-TSB.

Bonds. IOUs issued by companies and governments that can be traded in the financial markets, usually maturing after several years.

Bonus. A lump-sum addition to salary awarded for good performance, usually evaluated on an annual basis. An important feature of City remuneration that is catching on elsewhere.

Bourse. The French equivalent of the London Stock Exchange, also used as a general term for stock exchanges on continental Europe and elsewhere.

Building society. A mutually owned financial institution that takes deposits from its members and lends them out primarily for home purchase. In the UK many of the largest building societies of the 1980s are now banks.

Clearing. The mechanism by which retail banks and building societies settle their debts with each other at the end of the day.

Commercial bank. One that has a branch network and retail business.

Commercial paper. IOUs issued by companies or governments that can be traded in the financial markets, usually of one to six months' maturity.

Commodities. Basic physical assets that have market value, usually taken to mean agricultural products, metals, crude oil, or other raw materials.

CV. Curriculum Vitae, a Latin term (literally, course of life) taken to mean a summary of personal details, academic and other achievements, any career history, and a selection of hobbies and interests.

Derivatives. A general term for financial instruments for which the eventual value is determined by reference to the prices of securities, commodities, exchange rates, or agreed financial indices.

Exchange. When used on its own this is a designated place where financial instruments are traded.

Fast track. An accelerated training programme.

Foreign exchange. Currencies other than the domestic currency, sometimes shortened to 'forex'. Foreign exchange trading is speculating or managing risk in different currencies.

Fringe benefit. Compensation that is not counted as part of your salary but which has a financial value nevertheless.

Fund manager. A general term covering all those who manage large financial portfolios on behalf of groups of investors, pension funds or insurance companies.

Head-hunter. An employment agency or consultant.

Human resources. A long-winded way of saying personnel.

Investment bank. A bank that concentrates its activities on wholesale activities.

LIFFE. The London International Financial Futures and Options Exchange.

Lloyds. A corporation in the City that forms one of the world's largest insurance markets. It has nothing to do with banking and finance as defined in this book and is not to be confused with Lloyds Bank.

Local. A self-employed LIFFE trader, with his or her own capital at risk.

Marketing. In the context of banking this refers to the promotion of financial packages such as loans or foreign exchange services to potential customers.

MBA. Master of Business Administration, a postgraduate business degree.

Merchant bank. Another term for investment bank, usually applied to British investment banks. They often own stockbroking companies.

Middle office. A function that supports City trading desks by monitoring positions and calculating daily profit and loss.

Milk round. Annual presentations at universities by employers hoping to recruit graduates.

Money-broker. An intermediary in certain wholesale financial markets.

Multinational corporation. A company with operations in several countries.

Open outcry. An arrangement for trading that requires market participants to make public (open) agreements on quantity and price, in full view and hearing of other participants. The agreement can usually be made verbally (outcry) or by hand signal. It takes place on a recognised **exchange**.

Pit. That part of an exchange floor where all trading has to take place.

Portfolio. An assortment of financial assets, managed as a unit.

Retail sector. Banks and building societies that take deposits from, and lend money to, individuals and companies through a branch network. They may offer other services, such as stockbroking, financial advice, insurance, *etc*.

Securities. Financial obligations that can usually be freely bought and sold in financial markets, such as shares, bonds and commercial paper.

Shares. Certificates attributing part of the ownership of a public company to the owner. Traded in the stock market.

Stocks. A general term for shares *and* certain types of bonds. Often used wrongly as a synonym for shares alone.

Unit trust. A trust formed to manage securities on behalf of many investors, who each purchase a part (a unit) of the portfolio.

Wholesale sector. That part of the financial system that manages, trades, lends and borrows large amounts of money. It is also involved in advising large companies. In the UK this sector is concentrated in the City.

Work experience. Temporary employment for people still in education. Usually menial in nature, it can provide a valuable view of what a full-time job is like.

Further Reading

GENERAL CAREERS ADVICE

Applying for a Job, Judith Johnstone (How To Books, 3rd edition 1996).

GET 1998, Careers Research and Advisory Centre (Hobsons Publishing).

How to Start a New Career, Judith Johnstone (How To Books, 2nd edition 1997).

Passing That Interview, Judith Johnstone (How To Books, 4th edition 1997).

The Equal Opportunities Guide, Phil Clements and Tony Spinks (Kogan Page, 2nd edition 1996).

Which MBA? George Bickerstaffe, The Economist Intelligence Unit (Pitman, 9th edition 1997).

Writing a CV That Works, Paul McGee (How To Books, 2nd edition 1997).

FINANCIAL TERMS AND BACKGROUND INFORMATION

City Lives: The changing voices of British finance, Cathy Courtney and Paul Thompson (Methuen, 1997).

LIFFE: An introduction (LIFFE, 1995).

The Banker (monthly magazine).

The Financial Times A-Z of International Finance, Stephen Mahony (Pitman, 1997).

The Handbook of International Financial Terms, Peter Moles and Nicholas Terry (OUP, 1997).

The Money Machine: How the City works, Philip Coggan (Penguin, 3rd edition 1995).

DIRECTORIES

The Euromoney Bank Register 1998 (Euromoney Publications, 13th edition).

The Investor's Chronicle Directory of Stockbrokers and Investment Managers, Veronica McGrath (Pitman, 1990).

ENTERTAINMENT

All That Glitters: The Fall of Barings, John Gapper and Nicholas Denton (Penguin, 1996).

Liar's Poker: Two cities, true greed, Michael Lewis (Hodder, 1990).

Useful Addresses

Bank of England, Personnel Division, 1–2 Bank Buildings, Princes Street, London EC2R 8EU. Tel: (0171) 601 4518.

Building Societies Association, 2 Saville Row, London W1X 1AF.

Chartered Institute of Bankers, 901 Bishopsgate, London EC2N 4AZ.

Chartered Institute of Bankers in Scotland, 20 Rutland Square, Edinburgh EH1 2DE.

Commission for Racial Equality, Elliot House, 10–12 Allington Street, London SW1E 5EH. Tel: (0171) 828 7022.

Department of National Savings, Charles House, 375 Kensington High Street, London W14 8SD. Tel: 0645 645000.

Equal Opportunities Commission, Overseas House, Quay Street, Manchester M3 3HN. Tel: (0161) 833 9244 or (0171) 222 1110. For enquiries on sexual discrimination.

International Private Banking Council, Diana House, 4th Floor, 33–34 Chiswell Street, London EC1Y 4SE. Tel: (0171) 782 0590.

LIFFE, Cannon Bridge, London EC4R 3XX.

LIFFE Shop, Cannon Bridge, London EC4R 3XX. Tel: (0171) 379 2580.

For directories of financial institutions, see Further Reading.

Index

A-levels, 22, 23, 24, 25, 33, 45, 54, 63

academic qualifications, 21–25, 29, 30, 45, 63, 70, 72, 76, 90

addresses, 53, 78, 80

advertisements, 53, 55, 74, 75, 78, 80

application forms, 42, 55, 72, 76, 77, 79, 82, 83, 84, 88

Bank of England, 53–55, 56, 68, 72, 79, 81

banking certificate, 105

banking examinations, 46, 105–106, 107

big four, 42–43, 44, 45, 56, 66

bonds, 12, 51, 57, 60

bonus, 34

borrowing, 12, 13, 15, 59, 60

building societies
   in the City, 52, 65
   in the High Street, 16, 26, 28, 31, 32, 47–50, 55, 56, 59, 77, 78, 82, 85, 102, 105, 107
   role in the system, 11–16

Building Societies Act, 47

cashiers, 35

changing career, 9, 22, 26–29, 30, 65

Chartered Institute of Bankers, 46, 105–106

City, 58–73

applications to, 61–63, 66–68, 69, 71, 74, 75, 93

comparison with High Street, 14, 18, 28, 32–34, 35, 101, 105–106, 107

employer requirements, 21–24, 26, 29, 30, 31, 54, 58, 63–65, 72, 73, 79, 105–106

interviews, 85, 86

role in the system, 11–16, 18, 52, 59–60

salaries, 32–34, 41, 55, 99

clearing, 44

college, 45, 64

commercial banks, 66, 67, 72

communications, 24, 59, 60

computers, 14, 15, 16, 21, 24, 59, 61, 62, 81, 104

corporate finance, 24, 62, 63, 72

CV, 27, 30, 49, 53, 78, 79–80, 81, 82, 83, 84, 88, 93, 95, 100, 103

dealing, see trading

dealing rooms, 60, 63, 64, 68, 73, 89, 108

Department of National Savings, 55, 56

derivatives, 12, 60, 68, 69, 70

discrimination, 17–18, 86, 92

Docklands, 58

dress, 83–84, 88, 93, 103–104

employers, 9, 11, 21, 23, 26,

28–30, 39, 40, 58, 61, 64, 67, 72, 73, 75–77, 79–82, 83, 86, 88, 90, 91, 92, 94, 97–99, 101, 106, 107, 108
employment contracts, 20, 32, 45, 50, 100
English, 23, 24, 30, 54
enthusiasm, 28, 34, 40, 63, 65

Financial Services Authority, 54, 106
financial system, 11–16, 18, 26, 54, 57, 58, 71, 84, 93
Financial Times, 49, 51, 53, 57, 75
foreign banks, 43, 45–46, 55, 66–67
foreign exchange, 12, 51, 54, 59, 60, 68
fringe benefits, 41, 97
fund management, 12–14, 18, 51–53, 56, 57, 106, 107

GCSEs, 22–24, 25, 30, 33, 50, 54, 63, 92
graduates, 9, 63–65, 108
    recruitment, 22–23, 45, 50–53, 54, 56, 76
    salaries, 33, 41
    training, 46, 55, 105

head-hunters, see recruitment consultants
High Street, 42–57
    applications, 42, 44–46, 53, 54, 77, 79
    comparison with City, 14, 18, 28, 32–34, 35, 63, 65, 73, 101, 105–106, 107
    employer requirements, 21, 22, 28–30, 50–51, 54, 56, 58–59, 105
    interviews, 83, 86, 93

role in the system, 11–16, 18, 51
    salaries, 32–34, 99
hobbies, 25–26, 30, 37, 79
holidays, 26, 97
honesty, 38, 85–86, 88, 97, 101

insurance companies, 51–53
interviews, 20, 25, 27, 28, 31, 34, 36, 39, 45, 49, 63, 65, 74–78, 83–90, 91–96, 100, 102, 103, 104, 107
investment banks, 66, 69, 72
International Petroleum Exchange, 70

languages, 66
leisure, 33
letters, 49, 53
libraries, 49, 57, 74–75, 79, 82
London Commodity Exchange, 70
London International Financial Futures and Options Exchange (LIFFE), 68, 70–71, 72, 81, 88, 95, 101
London Metal Exchange, 70
London Stock Exchange, see stock market

management
    managers, 47, 64, 73, 87, 97, 99, 101, 103
    prospects, 16, 44–45, 46, 50, 66, 105
mathematics, 21, 23, 24, 29–30, 31, 50, 54, 79, 81
MBA, 23, 29, 30, 96
merchant banks, 66, 69
mergers, 47–49, 50, 62
milk round, 76
motivation, 32–41

newspapers, 26, 47, 55, 74, 75, 80, 82, 98, 101, 103

pension funds, 51
personnel, 57, 65, 73, 78, 80, 82, 86, 87, 89, 92, 98
Premium Bonds, 55
private banking, 43–44, 45–46, 55
professionalism, 50, 78, 85, 88, 95, 101, 104
promotion, 17, 50, 55, 56

recruitment consultants, 74, 76
redundancy, 15, 106–107
regulatory bodies, 106
rejection, 91–96
remuneration, 32–34, 35, 37–41, 73, 99, 101, 102
research, 22, 48, 52, 62, 63, 89, 91
retail sector, 12–14, 59, 66
retirement, 9, 31, 37

sales, 62–64, 72, 89, 102
saving, 12
school, 9, 21, 28, 45, 50, 83

school-leavers, 9, 26, 32, 58, 105
shares, 13, 59, 60, 68–69, 108
skills, 9, 16, 18, 21, 23, 27, 49, 58, 62, 76, 105
sponsorship, 54
sports, 35, 37, 91–92, 96, 108
standard letters, 78
stock market, 11, 12, 41, 68–69, 70, 73, 84, 108
stress, 33, 35, 36, 40, 41
support, 62–63, 72

The Economist, 49
trading, 13, 15, 35, 52, 60, 62–64, 69–71, 72, 73, 89
training, 16, 17, 18, 26, 29, 42, 45–46, 53, 55, 56, 57, 66, 89
unit trusts, 13, 51
university, 9, 21, 45, 58, 64, 76

vacancies, 53, 55, 74–77, 80, 81

wholesale sector, 12–14, 59, 60
women, 9, 17, 19, 64
work experience, 26, 45, 58, 107

PASSING THAT INTERVIEW
Your step-by-step guide to achieving success

Judith Johnstone

Using a systematic and practical approach, this book takes you step-by-step through the essential pre-interview groundwork, the interview encounter itself, and what you can learn from the experience. The book contains sample pre- and post-interview correspondence, and is complete with a guide to further reading, glossary of terms, and index. 'This is from the first class How To Books stable.' *Escape Committee Newsletter.* 'Offers a fresh approach to a well documented subject.' *Newscheck* (Careers Service Bulletin). 'A complete step-by-step guide.' *The Association of Business Executives.* Judith Johnstone is a Member of the Institute of Personnel & Development; she has been an instructor in Business Studies and adult literacy tutor, and has long experience of helping people at work.

144pp. illus. 1 85703 360 4. 4th edition.

GETTING YOUR FIRST JOB
How to win the offer of good prospects and a regular pay packet

Penny Hitchin

This readable handbook offers young people a real insight into what employers are looking for, encouraging the reader to take a constructive and positive approach to finding their first job. The book includes lots of practical examples, self-assessment material and typical case studies. Penny Hitchin has run Jobfinder programmes and has written careers books and materials for TV and radio campaigns on training and employment.

160pp illus. 1 85703 300 0.

WRITING A CV THAT WORKS
Developing and using your key marketing tool

Paul McGee

What makes a CV stand out from the crowd? How can you present yourself in the most successful way? This practical book shows you how to develop different versions of your CV for every situation. Reveal your hidden skills, identify your achievements and learn how to communicate these successfully. Different styles and uses for a CV are examined, as you discover the true importance of your most powerful marketing tool. Paul McGee is a freelance Trainer and Consultant for one of Britain's largest out-placement organisations. He conducts marketing workshops for people from all walks of life.

128pp. illus. 1 85703 365 5. 2nd edition.

APPLYING FOR A JOB
How to sell your skills and experience to a prospective employer

Judith Johnstone

Tough new realities have hit the jobs market. It is no longer enough to send employers mass-produced letters and CVs with vague details of 'hobbies and interests'. Employers want to know: 'What skills have you got? How much personal commitment? Will it be worth training you in the longer term?' This book shows you step-by-step how to tackle job applications, how to decide what you are really offering, and how to sell this effectively to your future employer. 'Very practical and informative.' *Phoenix* (Association of Graduate Careers Advisory Services). Judith Johnstone is a qualified local government administrator and Member of the Institute of Personnel & Development.

160pp. illus. 1 85703 245 4. 4th edition.

GETTING THAT JOB
The complete job finders handbook

Joan Fletcher

Now in its fourth edition this popular book provides a clear step-by-step guide to identifying job opportunities, writing successful application letters, preparing for interviews and being selected. 'A valuable book.' *Teachers Weekly*. 'Cheerful and appropriate . . . particularly helpful in providing checklists designed to bring system to searching for a job. This relaxed, friendly and very helpful little book could bring lasting benefit.' *Times Educational Supplement*. 'Clear and concise . . . should be mandatory reading by all trainees.' *Comlon Magazine* (LCCI). Joan Fletcher is an experienced Manager and Student Counsellor.

112pp. illus. 1 85703 380 9. 4th edition.

STAYING AHEAD AT WORK
How to develop a winning portfolio of work skills and attitudes

Karen Mannering

The world of work is changing and employers are demanding more than just qualifications. To stay employed it is vital that you build a flexible portfolio of skills that say more about how you work and interact with others, than just the job you do. Getting ahead is tough, staying ahead can be tougher still. This book includes techniques to help you develop that 'something special' that will give you the edge over colleagues. You will also learn how to develop transportable soft skills that will ensure your future employability. Karen Mannering has worked extensively in the field of personal development, helping people build up a portfolio of skills that will enhance their professional careers.

128pp. illus. 1 85703 298 5.